HENRY FORD

HENRY FORD

BY REGINA Z. KELLY

jacket painting by **HANK STALLWORTH**

illustrated with photographs

Follett Publishing Company *Chicago*

Other books by Regina Z. Kelly

Franklin D. Roosevelt

John Adams

John F. Kennedy

Marquette and Joliet

The author gratefully acknowledges the courtesy of the Ford Archives, Henry Ford Museum, Dearborn, Michigan, which permitted the reproduction of many photographs from their files. In addition, the author gratefully acknowledges the following organizations, which permitted the reproduction of photographs on indicated pages: Ford Motor Company, pp. 30, 44, 114, 127, 165; Wide World Photos, Inc., p. 169.

ISBN O 695-83702-8 Trade edition
ISBN O 695-43702-X Titan edition

Library of Congress Catalog Card Number: 68-14583

First Printing J

ACKNOWLEDGMENTS

I am deeply grateful for the assistance given to me by Mr. Henry E. Edmunds, Director of the Ford Archives, Dearborn, Michigan. In addition to carefully checking my manuscript for complete accuracy, Mr. Edmunds gave me additional valuable information about Henry Ford and his times. I appreciate, also, the help of Winfield Sears of the Ford Archives, who aided in the selection of the photographs for this book, and the assistance of the custodians of Fair Lane, Lovett Hall, and the buildings in Greenfield Village associated with the life of Henry Ford. They, too, shared little-known details of Ford's life with me. All librarians have my gratitude, but especially Mrs. Esther Loughin, who is the editor of *Michigan in Books* and a librarian in the Reference Library at Michigan State University.

R.Z.K.

Henry Ford at the age of two.

1

"Wheels in his head"

WILLIAM FORD WAS thoroughly angry when he strode into his farmhouse kitchen late on a fall day. John Miller, a neighboring farmer, had made a bitter complaint about Ford's ten-year-old son Henry. He and his friends had dammed a ditch near the schoolhouse with a "crazy contraption on wheels," and the water had spread all over Miller's potato patch.

"That boy has wheels in his head," shouted Mr. Ford to his wife, who was busy getting supper ready. "I'll lick him when he comes home."

Mrs. Ford only stirred the contents of a pot. Henry would probably not be home until suppertime. By then, her husband would be over his anger.

Near the schoolhouse, the boys were gloomily studying their broken device. Their only regret now was that Mr. Miller had destroyed their machine before they had had a chance to grind up big pieces of gravel.

Yesterday, after school, they had set up a waterwheel and hooked it to an old coffee mill. A rake handle connected the coffee mill and the wheel. Henry had supervised the work. His schoolmates were always eager to help him make something mechanical. They had tried it out with small pieces of clay and potatoes. But now the whole machine was broken.

Henry, however, was content that his small piece of machinery had actually worked. "We'll try something else," he said.

There was always "something else" on the farm with which Henry could "tinker," as his father said. He reset the handles of the farm tools. He repaired the harness and wagon. He had made a contrivance with which his father, when driving his wagon, could open and close the farm gates without getting out of the wagon.

All of this, Henry did willingly. He grumbled only when he had to work in the fields or in the farm buildings. "There's too much work on a farm," he would tell his father. "There are a lot of ways you could do it with less work."

Upstairs in his bedroom, Henry had a workbench with odds and ends of tools, many of which he had made himself. The tools were more fun for him than toys. Sometimes his father scolded him, but his mother always defended her oldest son. "Working with tools makes Henry happy," she told her husband. "If we can't be happy here in this house, we'll never be happy anywhere."

Somewhat reluctantly, Mr. Ford agreed to let Henry keep his workbench.

However, when Henry complained about a task, his mother insisted that he do it. "Life will give you many unpleasant things to do," she would tell him. "What you have to do might be hard or disagreeable, but you must do it."

Henry's mild-mannered mother, who never raised her voice or her hand to discipline him, would tell him, " 'I don't want to,' gets a fellow nowhere." And Henry would stop complaining and do his job.

Everything in the house must be neat and orderly, she told her family. It was a trait that Henry Ford never forgot. In later years, when he was complimented because his workshop and later his factory were neat, he would comment, "I learned that from my Dutch mother."

Mrs. Ford had told her sons about the Ford family and her own background. Three Ford brothers had come to America in 1832 from Cork, Ireland. They were English by birth, but had been tenant farmers for noblemen who had been given land in Ireland in 1585 by Queen Elizabeth I.

Samuel and George Ford bought land near the River Rouge in Dearborn Township, Michigan. Dearborn Township was just one day's journey by ox team from Detroit, which was eight miles to the west. It was on the Indian trail that connected Detroit with

Chicago, then becoming a thriving community. Dearborn Township had been named after General Henry Dearborn, a hero of the American Revolution and the War of 1812. Later, the third brother, Henry, went to California to search for gold.

In 1847, the oldest brother, John, came to Dearborn Township with his seven children and several other relatives. One of these children was William Ford, Henry's father. He was twenty years old at the time and a carpenter by trade.

The letters of the first arrivals had been full of the wonders and promise of the new land. At home in

Henry Ford's workbench in the bedroom of his reconstructed boyhood home in Greenfield Village.

Ireland, there had been a failure of the potato crop in 1847.

By this time, there were sixty families living in Dearborn Township. It had a sawmill, a foundry, and a smithy. A plank road would be built to Detroit in 1848, and not long after the Michigan Central Railroad would reach the little settlement.

The new arrivals were warmly welcomed. John Ford bought land, and his brothers and their children helped him to build a house and farm buildings. Cash was needed by the family while they cleared the land. William, John's oldest son, worked on the Michigan Central Railroad as a carpenter. But he liked farming best of all. In all his life, he was never to forget how wonderful it was for a man whose forefathers had been immigrants from Ireland to own his land.

In the later 1850's, William worked for Patrick O'Hern, an Irish immigrant, who owned a ninety acre farm nearby. The O'Herns had no children of their own, but they had adopted an orphan, Mary Litogot, whose parents had been Dutch or Belgian Flemish. Mary's father, a carpenter, had died in an accident. Her mother had died about the same time. She had three brothers, but the O'Herns had adopted only the little girl. Later in life, Henry Ford had exhaustive research made about his mother's ancestry, but these were all the facts he learned.

William Ford was attracted to Mary even though

she was fourteen years younger than he. By 1858, William owned his own farm in Springwells Township near Dearborn Township and could think of getting married. He and Mary were married on April 25, 1861.

The O'Herns liked William and were devoted to Mary. With the help of Patrick O'Hern, William built a two-story house with seven rooms. The Ford's first child died at birth. On July 30, 1863, their second child, Henry, was born in this house. This was an important month and year for the United States. It was a turning point in the Civil War, for the battles of Gettysburg and Vicksburg had been won by the North.

Other children were born after Henry, each about two years apart. John was born in 1865, and then came Margaret, Jane, William, and Robert. By this time, four more rooms had been added to the house. It was a simple but quite large white frame building. West of it was a small orchard, and on the other side were several farm buildings. A white picket fence separated the yard from the house. Nearby was the River Rouge, where the boys fished and swam.

The house was not only large but well furnished. Most of the family life was carried on in the sitting room back of the parlor and in the kitchen, though the dining room was used when the Fords had guests. The parlor was furnished in good black horsehair-covered chairs and settees, and had a large organ, which Mrs. Ford played.

The parlor of Ford's childhood home as reconstructed in Greenfield Village.

In later years, Henry Ford was able to remember distinctly the carpeting that covered the parlor floor in his boyhood home. So often, with freshly washed face and a clean blouse, he had sat on one of the slippery chairs and counted the roses in the carpet, as he fervently, though silently, wished the company would go home.

William Ford was an important member of the community by now. He was a warden in the church, a justice of the peace, and a member of the town council. He had an active interest in the affairs not only of his own village but of the whole country. Each day, he read his copy of the *Detroit Free Press* and a New York newspaper to which he subscribed.

When Henry was seven years old, he began attending the Scotch Settlement School, which was about a half mile from his home. He wasn't very happy about going to school, but he was not afraid. His mother had taught him to read from *McGuffey's First Reader,* and his schoolmates were the boys and girls from the neighboring farms. He also knew his teacher, Emilie Narden, a seventeen-year-old farm girl. First to greet Henry at school, was Edsel Ruddiman, who was a year younger than Henry.

The school was a one-room red brick building with desks and benches for the pupils, and the teacher's desk in front on a platform. In front of the room, facing the big black stove in the rear was the "mourner's bench" for those who misbehaved. Both Edsel and Henry spent much of their time on this bench. Edsel was a good student, but both boys were restless and full of mischief. Henry tried hard, but reading and spelling were difficult for him. He was good at arithmetic, however, and also at memorizing the poems in the McGuffey Readers.

Later, Henry attended the Miller School, where John B. Chapman was the teacher for the boys. Chapman was a big man who weighed 275 pounds. He was not well educated, but he had been hired for his weight and his strength, which would help him discipline the boys, rather than his book learning. Chapman kept the children grinding at their books from nine in the morning until four-thirty in the afternoon during the winter months. The rest of the year, Henry, like other boys, helped with the farm chores.

When Henry was twelve years old, his mother was expecting her eighth child. Mrs. Ford was still young and healthy. No one, including the doctor, thought there would be trouble. But the child died at birth. Twelve days later, on March 29, 1876, Mrs. Ford died.

For a time, the whole family was lost in grief, especially Henry, for his mother had been the center of his little world. Mr. Ford's sister managed the household for a time, and later on Margaret, Henry's oldest sister, was in charge. Henry never forgot the grief and emptiness of that first year without his mother. "The house was like a watch without a mainspring," he said later.

But there were other things that were to happen in the months that followed that also made Henry remember that year. In July, he was driving to Detroit with his father in their farm wagon. Suddenly ahead of them in the road, they saw a steam engine moving along. Henry stared. It was the first road vehicle not drawn by horses that he had ever seen. He had seen steam engines on a farm being used to supply power for threshing or sawing wood. But these machines had been pulled to the farm by horses.

The driver of the engine stopped to let the farm wagon pass, but Henry jumped down to the road. There were a dozen questions that he asked the engineer. How much horsepower did the engine have? How many times a minute did the wheels revolve?

"How do you know things like that?" asked the man, though he seemed pleased at the boy's interest.

Henry shook his head. He didn't know how he had acquired the information. But the questions he asked were about things he had always wanted to know.

That same month, on his birthday, William Ford gave Henry his first watch. Before nightfall, he had taken the watch apart to the anger and dismay of his father. But the next day, all the parts were in place again and the watch was running perfectly.

Although this was the first watch Henry had taken apart, he was confident that he could put it together again. When Henry was seven, one of the German immigrant farmhands who worked for his father had let Henry examine a watch for the first time. The man had explained how the watch worked. After that, whenever Henry's father had taken him to Detroit, he had spent his time with his nose pressed against the window of the jewelry shop, as he watched the jeweler repairing watches or clocks.

Not long after Henry received his first watch, Albert Hutchins, one of the boys at the Scotch Settlement Sunday School, came to the class with a watch fastened to a chain that crossed his vest. All of the boys looked enviously at Albert.

"But it doesn't run," said Henry, shaking the watch.

"I know," said Albert, looking embarrassed.

"I'll take it home and fix it for you," offered Henry.

"But you might ruin it," said Albert doubtfully.

"It doesn't run now," answered Henry.

At the carpenter shop of an uncle who lived nearby, Henry filed an old shingle nail until he had made a screwdriver small enough to use on the watch. He had already made a pair of tweezers from one of the stays in his mother's corset. With these tools, he was able to repair the watch. The next morning, he presented the smoothly running watch to Albert.

The news of this repair job spread in the little community. Soon Henry was busy with repair work for his neighbors.

"If you're going to fix every clock and watch around here, you ought to be paid," grumbled his father.

"But I'm learning something every time I do it," Henry protested. He was not interested in earning money.

"I still say you ought to get paid," insisted Mr. Ford.

So Henry, as much as he could, hid his work from his father, slipping out at night to a neighbor's to repair a clock or watch. Most of the tools that he used, he made himself—some from steel knitting needles.

There was one more important happening that year to make Henry remember it for something other than the death of his mother. In September, Mr. Ford and two of his neighbors went to Philadelphia to attend the Centennial Exposition. There was a special excursion rate of $2.50 from Detroit to Philadelphia. It was just one hundred years since the signing of the Declaration of Independence, and the exhibition halls in Philadelphia were filled with the machines that had been invented since that time.

The trip was not only exciting for the men but fascinating for Henry, as his father told him of the exhibitions. "We watched those engines and machines all day long," said Mr. Ford.

Henry's eyes glowed. If he had been in Philadelphia, he, too, would have been at the Exposition Hall each morning before the doors opened, and he would have stayed until they closed. Slowly over and over again, for there were many big words in the circulars Mr. Ford had brought home, Henry read the descriptions of the inventions and studied each line of the drawings. A new world had opened for him.

2

A young mechanic

IN THE FALL OF 1879, Henry told his father that he wanted to go to Detroit to get a job in a machine shop. At first, Mr. Ford objected. He had expected that Henry would help him on the farm now that he had finished school. In Mr. Ford's opinion, farming was the only way in which a man could become independent. But Henry hated farm work and was determined to become a mechanic.

Mr. Ford finally consented. He hoped that when Henry worked from dawn to dusk without a breath of fresh air in Detroit, he would realize that farming wasn't too bad.

There were over one hundred thousand people living in Detroit in 1879, and it covered almost seventeen square miles. The city had been carefully planned after a fire in 1807. The land sloped upward from the Detroit River, and fine homes surrounded by gardens and orchards were along the banks of the river. Already Detroit was a busy manufacturing and trading town. *De-troit* is the French word for strait, for the city was located on the narrow waterway that connected Lake Erie with Lake Huron. Detroit not only had fine water frontage, but ten railroads came to it from the United States and Canada.

By the time Henry came to Detroit, although the streets were still wide and tree-shaded, many of the fine old homes on the riverfront were gone, and more and more factories were being built. There were eighty miles of streets paved with wooden blocks or cobblestones. Lamps burning gas or oil lighted the street corners, and horse-drawn streetcars jangled along the main thoroughfares. The first telephones were being installed, and electricity was in use in the factories and stores.

Henry's first job was in the machine shop of the Michigan Car Company, where he was paid $1.10 a day, a high salary for the time. He was on this job only six days. He had repaired a machine in an hour, on which the experienced mechanics had already worked a day. Whether Henry angered the older men by this, or he left on his own account is not known. "I learned then not to tell all you know," he said later.

Henry soon got another job in the machine shop of the Flower Brothers. They were of English origin and friends of his father. He became an apprentice at $2.50 a week. However, as Henry was paying $3.50 a week for room and board, he supplemented his income by repairing watches in Robert Magill's jewelry shop.

Magill had been a neighbor of the Fords in Dearborn Township. Henry received fifty cents a night for four hours of work.

"But you'll have to work in the back of the shop and come in through the side door," Magill told him. "My customers won't leave their watches if they see them being repaired by such a young boy. You can use my jeweler's glass."

"I can see without it," said Henry. In all his work at Magill's, Henry never used a jeweler's glass. When he was seventy-seven years old, he was still able to repair a watch without using a jeweler's glass.

Henry worked for the Flower Brothers for only nine months. He was an apprentice there, and they believed in the English tradition of having an apprentice study each phase of a job before moving on to a new one. Henry knew that he was being thoroughly trained, but he wanted to learn more about different mechanical things. So he looked for employment elsewhere.

Although Henry was a poor reader, he had read every English and American magazine about mechanics that came to the shop of the Flower Brothers. There were articles about the development of engines that could be operated by the vaporizing of gas rather than by using steam. He was especially interested in this information, and hoped to learn more by getting other jobs.

Henry Ford during the period of his employment by the Detroit Drydock Company.

Henry's third job was with the Detroit Drydock Company, which was the largest shipbuilding firm in Detroit. There, he received training as a machinist, and he remained with the firm for over two years. Although he was making more money now, he still continued to repair watches in the evening.

A plan for producing watches in large numbers ran through his mind as he worked at Magill's. He figured he could make a watch to sell for thirty cents, if he could make two thousand in a day. However, he realized that a watch was a luxury, and he didn't think enough people would buy watches to make the price possible. "I have to make something in quantity that is a necessity," he decided.

In each of the three years Henry worked in Detroit, he would go home in the spring and summer to help his father on the farm. After the spring of 1882, Henry remained at the farm. However, he worked only part time for his father. His brother John was eighteen now and William was twelve, so that they could help with the farm work. Henry planned to spend much of his time repairing farm machinery, like the engine he had seen on the road that July day in 1876.

That summer, a neighboring farmer, John Gleason, bought a portable steam engine from Westinghouse to do threshing and wood sawing on his farm. Gleason hired a man to operate the machine, but the man knew so little about steam engines that he was afraid to operate it.

Another neighbor, who was aware of Henry's mechanical ability, came early in the morning to the Ford farm and asked Mr. Ford to let Henry operate the machine. Mr. Ford consented reluctantly, for he knew that Henry had never operated a Westinghouse steam engine. Although Henry knew that the Westinghouse was a "little high-speed, quick-steaming thing," and he was somewhat nervous about handling it, he was eager to take the job.

Henry was weary and dirty at the end of the day, but he had run the engine smoothly and efficiently. A delighted Farmer Gleason paid him three dollars for the day's work. Henry had eighty-three days work that summer at the same rate, as he traveled from one farm to another operating Gleason's machine. At the end of the summer, Henry was hired by Westinghouse to demonstrate their machines.

Henry did no other farm work after this. In the summers, he demonstrated the Westinghouse engines. In the winter, he made experiments in his own workshop on the farm. As he worked, he thought about producing power for the engine he was designing. On the farms, he used wood for fuel because coal was too expensive. Electricity or gasoline he realized would be

John Gleason's machine, restored at Greenfield Village.

much better, but he knew nothing about how to use either one.

Wood as a fuel for a steam engine was a big problem for everyone, although it was cheap and available. It was quickly consumed by the fire for a steam engine. In addition, one had to wait until the water boiled long enough to produce steam. Gasoline would be lighter to transport, but the first oil wells in the United States had been dug only a little more than twenty years before. In the beginning it was used only for lamps, and gasoline, as we know it today, was not being manufactured.

In the winter of 1884, Henry started going back and forth to Detroit to take courses at a business school. On July thirtieth of that year, the day on which Henry was twenty-one years old, his father offered him a piece of land.

"If you give up the idea of being a machinist, you can move to that forty acre piece of timberland west of my farm," said Mr. Ford. "If you cut the timber, the land is yours."

"I'm not sure I want to do that, Pa," said Henry. "But I'll cut the timber and clear the land."

In a few months, Henry was less anxious to return to Detroit. On New Year's Eve in 1885, at a dance given by the Greenfield Dancing Club at the Martindale House, he met Clara Jane Bryant, who lived in nearby Greenfield Township. She was eighteen at the time, and the oldest of ten children of a farmer, Melvin B. Bryant. Clara was a small, pretty girl, with dark hair and eyes, and she was an excellent dancer.

Henry liked Clara immediately and danced several times with her that night. But it was nearly a year later before he met Clara again at a dance. He told his sister Margaret about his interest in Clara, which pleased Margaret, for Clara was one of her best friends. She warned Henry, however, that Clara was popular and had many beaux. From that time on, Henry began to devote more time to dancing and parties, and started to court Clara Bryant. His sisters, Margaret and Jane, had taught him to dance and he found he enjoyed it. The large halls where the parties were held were lighted with candles and oil lamps. A musician called off the dances as he played, and the young people danced polkas and reels.

That winter, Henry built a red sleigh with cushions and springs to take Clara riding. They also went to many dances together. In the summer, he took her for buggy rides on the country roads. They went to Detroit to see a minstrel show, and several times they had dinner at the Martindale House, where they had first met.

Henry Ford was a nice-looking young man now. He was medium of height and thin, but wiry and strong. He could walk and run faster, leap over fences higher, and skate on the ice of the River Rouge better than almost anyone he knew. His eyes were bright blue, with rather dark, heavy eyebrows. His hair was dark and curly and parted a little to the left. His features were firm and straight.

As time went on, Ford became more and more attracted to Clara Bryant. He even went to church with her, though he was not religious. But Clara Bryant was an Episcopalian and attended church regularly. What Henry liked best about her was that she was a good and intelligent listener. She never seemed bored when Ford talked about the mechanical things in which he was interested.

"I'm sure you're going to do something that's important," she told him, and his heart was warmed by her firm belief in him. He was convinced by now, that even if he had to continue living in Dearborn, he would never be happy unless Clara Bryant married him. They became engaged on April 19, 1886, but Clara's mother thought her twenty-year-old daughter was too young to marry then. So Henry Ford waited two more years for his bride.

Clara Bryant and Henry Ford were married in the Bryant's large brick house on April 11, 1888. The wedding invitations had a silver spray of leaves and blossoms at the top. An Episcopalian minister presided. Ford wore a dark blue suit, and Clara Bryant was dressed in a gown that she had made herself. There was a houseful of guests for the wedding supper, but

Clara Bryant and Henry Ford at the time of their marriage.

it was simple, though plentiful.

"Well, Henry's settled now with a good wife who likes a farm," Mr. Ford told his family. "Maybe, he'll be content to stay."

In the months that followed, Ford continued to cut his timber. Much of it he sold. Some he milled and seasoned for the home he and his wife planned. Until it was built, they lived in a small house on the land. The new house was a story and a half high, painted white, and square in shape, thirty-one feet each way. Ford's workshop was attached to the house. The turned balustrades around the porches on the first and second floor and the top of the square-shaped roof were made by a good carpenter. Mrs. Ford furnished their home with pieces of family furniture, but they bought an organ, for Clara Ford liked to play.

Ford did no farming on his land.

In his workshop, he repaired machinery for himself and his neighbors and experimented with steam and gas engines. One evening he talked to Clara about building a "horseless carriage." In spite of her belief in her husband's ability, she was astonished at the idea.

"But what would a horseless carriage look like?" she asked.

"Get me a piece of paper, and I'll show you," he said.

She handed him a sheet of music from the organ rack. Ford began to draw on the blank side, explaining as he drew.

"I can see how it would work," said Clara. "I am sure you can build it." All through her life with Henry Ford, Clara Ford believed implicitly in his ability to do what he planned. In time, the family teasingly called her, "The Believer."

Though Henry Ford was busy making a good income, he became restless on the farm. Occasionally, he went to Detroit to do some repair work. In the late summer of 1891, a little over three years after they were married, he suggested to his wife that they move to Detroit. "I can get a job there, and I can build my horseless carriage," he said.

Clara turned her head so that her husband would not see the disappointment in her face. To go to Detroit

The Ford's second home, as restored in Greenfield Village.

to live meant giving up the farm life she loved, and separation from her family and friends. They were secure on the farm. What would be their prospects in Detroit?

She bit her lips to hide their trembling. "If that's what you want, Henry, we'll go to Detroit," she said, "as soon as you get the job."

"I've been offered a job already as night engineer at the Edison Illuminating Company," he said. He was too full of joy to notice the tears in his wife's eyes.

On September 25, 1891, Henry and Clara Ford rode off to Detroit in a hay wagon piled high with their furniture. As the wagon started, Clara turned for one last look at the white, square-shaped house in which she had been so happy. She thought it was the prettiest house she had ever known.

3

The horseless carriage

THE FIRST HOME of the Fords in Detroit was in an apartment on John R. Street, a few blocks from the Edison plant. Ford worked twelve hours at night for forty-five dollars a month. This was more than he had averaged on his farm, but the cost of living was higher in Detroit. In 1892, he was engaged to teach a metal-working class at the Y.M.C.A. He was paid $2.50 a night for this. More important for Henry than the extra money he earned was the fact that he could use the Y.M.C.A. machine shop for his own metal work.

Since their move to Detroit, Henry had continued with his experiments to make a horseless carriage. Sometimes he was hard pressed for money, though all that could be spared from his salary was used to buy tools and material. Clara Ford never complained. Her only concern was that there would not be enough money on hand at a time when her husband was in urgent need of something.

In 1893, Ford acquired a camera and a bicycle. Bicycles were new and exciting vehicles in the nineties, though used for the most part to get around in the cities. In the country, there were mainly rough wagon roads.

However, as the craze for bicycling grew, people began to realize how poor the roads were outside the cities. There was much urging of public officials to improve the roads, and probably, because of his interest in bicycling, Ford was one of the most insistent. He and his family liked nothing better than a picnic in the country.

Henry Ford and his bicycle.

Ford's little camera also was a great source of pleasure for him. He took several pictures of his numerous homes, and of his friends, but most of the photographs were of his family. He also photographed the places he visited and the people he met.

By 1895, horseless carriages were in operation both in Europe and the United States. They were operated by steam and electricity as well as gasoline. Charles and Frank Duryea, who were bicycle makers in Springfield, Massachusetts, built the first American gasoline car. Their first successful run was on or about September 20, 1893.

Other men began manufacturing cars. A few were sold, but no manufacturer was able to get enough financial backing to produce automobiles on a large scale. Besides the Duryea brothers, cars were made by Ransom E. Olds, the Haynes-Apperson Company, Alexander Winton, and Hiram Maxim.

Henry Ford continued to improve his position at the Edison Company. On December 1, 1893, just weeks after his son Edsel's birth on November 6, Henry was promoted to chief engineer of the Edison Company at a salary of one hundred dollars a month.

In the middle of December, 1893, the Fords moved to a two-family house at 58 Bagley Street. This was the seventh home to which they had moved. They were to stay there until the middle of 1897.

A shed to store wood and coal was in back of the

house on Bagley Street. Soon Ford moved the fuel into the kitchen and used the shed for his experiments. His neighbor, Felix Julien, was a friendly old man who was retired. He became so interested in what Ford was doing that Julien also moved his fuel into his kitchen so that Ford would have more room to work. All that Julien asked was the privilege of sitting in the doorway of the shed to watch Ford at work.

On Christmas Eve that year, Clara Ford was busy at the sink in her kitchen getting the turkey ready for dinner next day when Ford came into the room with the engine he had built.

"I want to try out my engine," he said. "I'll have to clamp it to a platform over the sink. I can use the house current for a spark plug."

Clara gave a little sigh. Heaven only knew when she'd get the turkey ready. But Ford didn't even notice; he was so busy with the engine. Then he connected a wire from the kitchen light to the spark plug.

"While I spin the wheel to start the engine, I want you to feed the intake valve by hand with gasoline from this oil can," he instructed his wife. "If the engine will run, I can design the rest."

Carefully, Ford showed Clara how she could feed the valve by turning a screw. With eyes intent, and steady hand, she prepared to follow her husband's directions. The only sound in the kitchen now was the ticking of the big wall clock. Both watched almost breathlessly.

34

Drop by drop the gasoline fell. Ford turned the fly-wheel. The air and gasoline were sucked into the cylinder. The kitchen light flickered for a second. Ford gave the wheel another turn. The engine coughed and roared into action. The kitchen sink shook with the vibration. Flames shot from the exhaust. Clara Ford gave a frightened gasp.

"It's all right," said Ford. "Don't be scared." The wheel was revolving now by itself, the sink still shaking as the engine operated.

For another minute, Ford watched, then stopped the engine. "It will work," he said quietly, but his eyes showed his elation.

Clara Ford gave a big sigh of relief.

"Now you can finish the turkey," said Ford as he unclamped the engine. "All I wanted to find out was would it work."

Right after the test at the kitchen sink on Christmas Eve, Ford began to build an engine powerful enough to run a horseless carriage. Often until midnight, he worked in the shed of the house on Bagley Street. Rough wooden cabinets filled with tools lined the grimy, unfinished walls. A vise and other tools were on a corner shelf. There was a potbellied stove, and electric lights with tin reflectors hung from the ceiling. Because he often was called for some special emergency at the Edison plant, Ford had an extension telephone in the shed.

There were usually other men in the shed with

Ford, for he had no trouble getting people to help him. All his life, Henry Ford seemed to have this special ability. Men like Jim Bishop and Edward Huff, who worked at the Edison plant with him, spent their evenings and holidays giving Ford a hand or making suggestions, some of which were valuable. Old Felix Julien, as a rule, lingered in the doorway until his bedtime to see what was going on. On Saturday nights, there was quite a crowd. Ford liked company and was cheerful, talkative, and friendly.

Mrs. Ford would come into the shop when he was

58 Bagley Street.

alone or working with one or two men. She would sit on a high stool and knit or sew as she watched her husband working. When neighboring women called in the evening, Mrs. Ford would leave them now and then, though she never told them why. "Henry is making something," she would say. "Maybe, some day I'll tell you about it."

Henry Ford was not the only one in the United States working on a design for a horseless carriage. There were about three hundred inventors trying to solve this problem. They knew little about each other's experiments. Not much was written either in newspapers or magazines about their developments. Nothing was taught in technical schools. No patents for a vehicle operated by an internal combustion engine had been issued except the one issued to George B. Selden in May, 1879. However, he changed his device a number of times and did not get his final patent until May, 1895. The inventors, most of whom were good mechanics, had various motives for designing their vehicles. One man said he started inventing a self-propelled vehicle because he had a bicycle and he was tired of using his legs to propel it.

Steam engines had been used for locomotion both in England and the United States since early in the nineteenth century. Although experiments in developing internal combustion or "gas engines" had started as early as 1774, it was 1860 before the first successful gas engine was patented by a Belgian, Jean Lenoir, who was living in Paris at the time.

Two Germans, Nicholas Otto and Eugene Langen, designed another gas engine that was an improvement on the Lenoir engine because it was more economical to run. It went into production in 1872. An Otto engine was on exhibit in Philadelphia in 1876, and, no doubt, was seen by William Ford.

About the same time, George B. Brayton, an Englishman living in Boston, also patented a gas engine. Although the Brayton engine was not as good at first as the Otto engine, it became the one used by American manufacturers of automobiles. The Otto engine was most widely used in European cars.

From about 1870, work was also being done in Europe in designing a carriage to be propelled by a gas engine. Except for the Otto engine, little was known in America about any of these developments.

Gustave Daimler and Karl Benz developed a gas-propelled vehicle by 1886, but because of lack of funds did not go into production until 1892. Their carriage was produced and sold then by a French company under Emile Levassor. There was rapid progress after this, for the roads of France were level and smooth, and far better for automobile traffic than in the United States. The Daimler and Mercedes-Benz are still high quality luxury cars produced in Europe today.

The first car races took place in France in 1894 and

1895. Because manufacturing of gas-propelled vehicles had started in France, many of the terms connected with the automobile that are still common today are French such as garage, chauffeur, and chassis.

Meanwhile in the United States, Charles and Frank Duryea, Ransom E. Olds, Hiram Maxim, and Elwood Haynes were working on designs for a horseless carriage. All except Olds were unknown to the public. Few people knew what was happening in Europe.

Finally the Duryea brothers had the first trial run of their car on September 20, 1893. Not long after, the Duryea Motor Wagon Company was formed. Elwood Haynes completed his car in 1894. Olds and Maxim soon followed. By 1895, carriages propelled by gasoline motors were in actual operation not only in Europe but in the United States.

About this time, Henry Ford met Charles Brady King, a young, well-educated engineer, who already had several profitable inventions on the market. King was also interested in designing a horseless carriage, and he and Ford became friends. They read articles and exchanged information and were interested in each other's experiments.

A big incentive for the inventors in the United States was the announcement of the first American race for horseless carriages to be held on Thanksgiving

Day, November 28, 1895. The race was to be run from Jackson Park in Chicago to Evanston, Illinois, and back, a total distance of fifty-two miles. It was sponsored by Herman B. Kohlsaat, the publisher of the *Chicago Times-Herald*. Prizes were from five hundred to two-thousand dollars. King's car was not ready for the event, but he was named the umpire for one of the entries, a Benz car. An umpire rode with the driver and kept track of the time, distance, and so on.

Six cars entered the race, but only two cars completed the full course. The day was bitter cold, and there was a heavy snowfall, so that the road was filled with ruts and about a foot of snow.

The race started at 8:55 in the morning. Only the Duryea and the Benz cars finished. Frank Duryea came in at 7:18 in the evening. It had taken him ten hours and twenty-three minutes to travel the fifty-two miles, an average speed of 6.66 miles an hour. The Benz car, with King as the umpire, finished one hour and forty-five minutes later. The driver had collapsed, and King had to drive the last part of the course with one arm, as he held up the driver with the other. When King returned to Detroit, he told Ford all the details of the event.

On March 6, 1896, King was the first one to test a horseless carriage in the streets of Detroit. The test was made at night and was reported in the *Detroit Free Press*. "It was a most unique machine," wrote the reporter.

Behind the machine, as it moved through the dark streets, rode Henry Ford on a bicycle. He had developed his own engine by this time, but he was eager to see how a vehicle propelled by gasoline actually worked. This was the first one he had seen in operation.

Ford had his own car on wooden horses by the end of 1895, and was now working on details. King's car was a wagon using the engine he had designed. Ford was designing both engine and car. He had definite requirements for his car. It must be light in weight, rugged, simple in design, and most important of all, it must be dependable.

By the end of May, 1896, Ford's car was almost

Clara Ford and her son Edsel dressed in his father's vest. Photograph taken by Henry Ford.

ready for a trial. The carriage was mounted on four bicycle wheels, twenty-eight inches in diameter, and having rubber tires. There was a tiller to steer it, and a warning electric doorbell was fastened to the front. A button in the top of the tiller rang the bell. The transmission was a belt from the motor to the rear wheels.

The car had two speeds, and four horsepower, and Henry thought it would go about twenty-five miles an hour. King's car would go only five miles an hour. Ford's car had no brakes. He stopped it by killing the engine. Neither did the car have a reverse. If he wanted to go backward, Henry expected to get out and push the car back. He expected to use a buggy seat big enough for two people, but for the trial he planned to use a bicycle seat.

"I'm going to try out my horseless carriage early tomorrow morning," Ford told his wife on June 3. She gave him a worried look. He had been working so hard on the car that he had hardly slept for the past two nights.

About two o'clock the next morning, Henry was ready with his car. Clara Ford, who had sat up all night, hurried out to the shed with an open umbrella and a shawl over her head, for a light, warm rain was falling. Jim Bishop was in the shed with Ford.

"I'm ready now," said Ford. "Open the door, Jim."

The door was opened. The light from the shed lit up the dark yard. Both men gave the vehicle a push, then stopped short. The carriage was too big to go through the open door.

"Oh, Henry!" cried Clara in dismay.

"I'll fix that," said Ford. He picked up an axe and began to knock down the thin wall of brick next to the door, and then part of the door frame. Jim Bishop helped him. In a short time, the opening was wide enough for the car to be pushed through.

Ford turned on the house electric current for the battery and adjusted the gasoline. Then he covered the intake valve with his thumb and forefinger to choke it, then turned over the flywheel. The engine sputtered, then roared. Ford mounted the seat and slowly bumped over the cobblestones of the narrow alley between his house and the building next door, until he emerged on Bagley Street. Mrs. Ford and Jim Bishop ran after him.

Carefully Ford steered his carriage. Jim Bishop had jumped on his bicycle and had ridden ahead. The streets were dark and quiet. Jim Bishop did not even meet a milk wagon. No one heard or saw what they were doing. Wide-eyed and scarcely breathing, Mrs. Ford watched until the little vehicle turned on Grand River Avenue and disappeared from her sight.

Along Grand River Avenue went the two riders. Suddenly the car stopped. Ford called to Bishop, who was not far in advance. The two men examined the engine. A spring had failed. In a few minutes, they had pushed the car to the nearby Edison plant and gotten a new spring.

By this time, a small group of people coming from a party in a neighboring hotel had gathered around the car.

"What kind of a crazy contraption is this?" asked a man.

But Ford and Bishop paid no attention as they made their repairs. Once more Ford started the engine, then jumped into the car. Jim Bishop ran for his bicycle and rode ahead. Around the block and back to 58 Bagley Street they traveled. Henry Ford's first car had made a successful run.

Early the next morning, Ford hired two bricklayers

Henry Ford and his first automobile, which he called a quadricycle.

to repair the damage to the wall of his shed. Just as the men began to work, the owner of the house called to collect the June rent. He was angry when he saw the broken wall.

"What did you do?" he cried.

"I had to knock it down to get my car out," said Ford.

"You mean you ran it!" said the man in amazement, for he also had watched Ford at work. "Let me see."

Ford showed him the car and related what had happened. In his excitement, the landlord forgot about the broken wall. "I have an idea," he said. "Don't build that wall. Put in a swinging door, and then you can always get the car out." And so this may have been the first swinging garage door in the United States.

It was not long before Ford put a buggy seat in the car and took his wife for a ride, as she held Edsel on her lap. With scarcely a word to each other at first, but smiling confidently at the end, the little family drove around the block.

4

The Detroit Automobile Company

HENRY FORD'S FIRST long ride was to his father's farm. Clara sat on the seat with her husband, holding tightly to Edsel. The whole family in Dearborn was interested and excited.

Only Ford's father refused to take a ride that day. "I can't see why I should risk my life," he said, "just to get the thrill of riding in a carriage without a horse."

After this, Ford frequently rode around the streets of Detroit. Jim Bishop usually rode ahead on his bicycle, even entering stores to warn people to hold their horses. Whenever Ford got out of the car and left it for a short time, a crowd gathered. Occasionally, someone tried to start the car, so in time Ford carried a chain and padlock with him to fasten the car to a lamppost.

Ford still continued to work for the Edison Company. In August, 1896, he went with his boss, Alex Dow, to New York for a convention of illuminating companies. He met a number of important men, but his greatest thrill was meeting and talking to Thomas

Alva Edison at the closing banquet of the convention.

The men at the table with Ford began to talk about how and where to charge storage batteries for electric vehicles, which were now being used in the cities.

"Here's a young man who has made a gas car," said Dow to the group, as he pointed to Ford.

"How do you make your car go?" asked someone.

Ford started to explain. He spoke as loudly as he could so that Edison, who was several seats away, could hear, for he knew that the inventor was hard of hearing. Then a man offered Ford the seat next to Edison. On the back of a menu, Ford sketched his car for Edison, explaining as he drew.

"Young man," said Edison, thumping his fist on the table, "you have it. You don't have to carry water and coal for steam, and you don't have to be near a place to charge your batteries. You have a unit that carries its own fuel. Keep at it."

This was the greatest moment in Henry Ford's life up to that time. From then on, Edison was his idol.

Ford had brought his camera to the convention, and he took pictures of the notables present and the interesting things he saw. Both Charles B. Steinmetz and Samuel Insull were there, but Ford's chief interest was in photographing Edison. He took one picture of Edison napping in a porch chair. Ford probably grinned at this. "Never to bed," was Edison's slogan, and he claimed he slept little at night or not at all.

Most people knew, however, that Edison took naps everywhere and used anything for a pillow.

Ford began working on a second car after he came home from the convention. He had sold his first car for about $200 to Charles Ainsley, who was a close friend and the nephew of one of the wealthiest men in Detroit. This was the first sale of a used car. In the spring of 1897, Ainsley sold the car, which was still in good working condition, to a man in Cleveland. The second owner wrote Ford a glowing letter of recommendation, and said he was in the market for another car if Ford produced it.

The second car was far better and much sturdier than the first one. Ford worked slowly, for he was constantly experimenting. "Let's see what would happen if . . ." he would say. He would try any idea, either his

Henry Ford's photograph of Thomas Edison napping at Atlantic City.

own or another man's, if he thought the car could be improved.

About a year after the convention, the Fords moved into their eighth rented home. They moved frequently. In all, they lived in eleven rented houses before they built their own home in Detroit.

Moving from one small house to another was not so difficult or expensive then. Friends helped, and a local mover could be hired for a small amount. Once the Fords paid $3.50 to have all their furniture, including their piano, moved from one house to another. In 1895, Mrs. Ford had forty-two yards of carpet cleaned for $1.26, or three cents a square yard, and she paid $10 to have a couch re-covered.

Several of the houses in which the Fords lived were on narrow lots. Clara, it would appear at this time, evidently took little interest in a garden or lawn, for a number of snapshots of their houses showed poorly kept lawns. However, in the eighth house, the Fords, to have their "lawn neatly mowed and rolled from Spring until October 1," paid a gardener $1.50.

As Ford built his second car, he was thinking of manufacturing it for sale. However, he wanted to take steps gradually and get proper financing before starting production. Other inventors had started immediately, and most of them had failed. Only the Duryea brothers so far had produced a real car for sale, and they were having financial trouble. But Henry knew that soon Alexander Winton's car would be in production, and in a year or two, Ransom E. Olds would begin manufacturing his Oldsmobile.

A few days after Ford had taken his first ride in his car, William C. Maybury, the Mayor of Detroit, had come around to Bagley Street to take a ride. The Mayor's father, Thomas C. Maybury, was a close friend of William Ford. Henry Ford's parents had been married in the home of Thomas Maybury.

The Mayor was enthusiastic about Henry's car and gave him an oral permit to drive. This was the first driver's license given in the United States, though it was only a verbal permission to drive on the streets of Detroit. Maybury spoke enthusiastically to his friends, many of whom were prominent businessmen, about the good points in Ford's car and why it should be produced for sale. On August 5, 1899, Maybury and about two dozen businessmen organized the Detroit Automobile Company to manufacture the cars that Henry Ford designed.

By this time, the Detroit Edison Company was ready to expand and Ford was offered the job of superintendent. However, he would have to give all of his time and attention to his new job. Instead, he decided to resign, and did so on August 15, 1899. Almost at once, he became the superintendent of the newly formed Detroit Automobile Company. "I had to choose between my job and the automobile. I chose the automobile," said Ford later. By this time, he had applied for a patent on his car and had assigned it to Maybury.

Manufacturing for the Detroit Automobile Company was carried on in a large, well-lighted plant on Cass Avenue. It had more working space than Ford had ever known. The company expected to manufacture one hundred and fifty cars a year.

Ford tried to induce some of the men in the Edison plant who had helped him so willingly in the past to go to the new plant with him. But all of them refused. They had families to support and their present jobs were secure. They had faith in Ford but not in his car. "He had the dream," they said, but to them Ford's car was only a "dream."

Progress of the company was slow. In the first year, only three cars were made. This was mainly because the parts were difficult to obtain, and most of the work was done by hand. The men assembling the cars had little experience. The heavier parts were manufactured elsewhere, and there were delays in their shipment. Even the small parts were frequently the wrong size, and this meant much drilling, riveting, and bolting by hand to make the parts fit. To the workmen, the number of separate parts both in the engine and the body of the vehicle seemed overwhelming.

In addition, Ford himself delayed progress, for he was never satisfied with the result and was constantly making changes. The first car was ready, though not

Interior of the Detroit Automobile Company plant.

as early as expected, by January 12, 1900. It was in the form of a delivery wagon and was expected to be used to deliver mail. The price was $1000.

Ford did not want to go into production until he had a car that satisfied him. His backers were men who were used to making money quickly. He made a fourth car, which was better than the third, but he was still not satisfied. By 1901, Olds was producing 425 Oldsmobiles a year, and selling every one of them.

The Detroit Automobile Company dissolved in January, 1901. Although the backers had lost $86,000 in the enterprise, they engaged Ford to continue with his experiments. Maybury had stuck with him until the end, buying up the stock of the other investors as they withdrew from the company. The real fault for the failure of the company had been with Ford himself. He had made his new models too slowly, and when the fourth model was finished, it was not a good car.

The Fords continued their simple way of life, though their income and prestige had risen. They were a devoted family. In spite of his constant experiments, Ford found time to play with his son. He gave Edsel many toys, including a rocking horse and a late model tricycle with a wide wooden seat. He repaired Edsel's sled and took him coasting and made a toboggan slide for him in their backyard. No doubt, he taught Edsel to skate, for Ford was an excellent skater himself.

Ford took many pictures of his wife and son with his camera. Mrs. Ford also learned to use the camera and took numerous snapshots of Edsel, whose every move and thought was of constant interest to his parents. There were studio pictures, too, of Edsel as a baby in long dresses, and later on in a good sailor suit or full ruffled white blouse, with his curls carefully arranged. Edsel was a quiet, sweet baby, and he retained something of these traits all his life.

Clara Ford kept a diary and wrote a few lines almost every day about their simple home life. Many of the entries were about Edsel. She wrote of the new salad dressing she had made, which was "licking good." She told of meeting her husband going home on the streetcar, or having dinner with him downtown.

Rarely was there a reference to an important event. On January 22, 1901, she wrote. "Queen Victoria died today. Cut out dressing sack for myself."

Both the Fords liked music, and Henry Ford always enjoyed the simple tunes that his wife played. In place of the organ, he bought a player piano, paying for it on the installment plan. Ford's credit must have been good, for in 1901 he was still paying on the piano. "We had a little music tonight," was frequently written in Clara's diary.

The Fords also loved the theater. Mrs. Ford took Edsel to see *Little Lord Fauntleroy,* and she and her husband went to see *The Old Homestead,* the most popular melodrama of the time. Most of the leading actors and actresses came to Detroit on tour and always played to a full house. Ethel Barrymore and her brother John came, though in different plays. George M. Cohan, Eddie Foy, Sarah Bernhardt, Maude Adams, and Ellen Terry also performed in Detroit early in the twentieth century.

Except when he was in the shop, where he wore a long work coat over his clothes, Henry Ford was always well dressed. He wore a dark suit with a vest, a high-collared shirt with a bow tie, and a black derby hat. These were the typical clothes for a man in the executive class at the time, the quality and cut depending on his wealth and importance.

About 1892, Ford began growing a big black

moustache. He shaved this off in 1903, and was clean-shaven for the rest of his life. His curly dark hair was beginning to gray then, but he was proud of his hair and gave it good attention. Although it grew thinner as he grew older, he was never bald. He always remained thin, and his cheeks looked rather sunken at times.

Clara Ford dressed well, though she made most of her own clothes. She wore the high-necked shirtwaists and long, full skirts that were fashionable at the time, and the rather masculine looking straw sailor or felt hats with turned-up brims.

The Fords were an affectionate couple and never failed to show their love for each other. When her husband was away, Clara Ford frequently visited her family in Greenfield Township. In her letters to her husband, she told him how she missed him and wished that he would be home soon.

"Darling husband," she began her letter when he was away at the convention in New York. "I hope things will be all right at the station," she ended the letter, "so that you can come out, for I want you awful bad. Dearest husband, goodbye, Clara."

Clara Ford's spelling and punctuation were far superior to her husband's. Although he found writing difficult, he would reply. Once when away, he even wrote to Edsel. He printed the words in the letter so that the little boy, who was just beginning to go to school, could read the letter for himself.

MY DEAR LITTLE SON
    I AM WELL AND HOPE YOU ARE ALL
O K. . . . I HOPE YOU ARE HAVING A GOOD TIME
AND WILL BE BACK SOON FOR I AM LONESOME.
FROM YOUR LOVING
PAPA.

By 1901, after the failure of the Detroit Automobile Company, Henry Ford was out of a regular job, but he had experience as well as strong faith in his ideas, and a wife who shared that belief. With the financial help of some of his backers from the Detroit Automobile Company, he still continued his experiments in the shop on Cass Avenue.

Although the Fords were not short of money, to economize they lived with William Ford and his daughter Jane, who had moved to Detroit. Margaret Ford had married James Ruddiman, the brother of Edsel Ruddiman, Ford's boyhood schoolmate, after whom the Fords had named their son. Now Jane was keeping house for her father.

By 1901, there were fifty-seven companies in the United States making cars, although on a small scale. No city as yet was the center of the industry. However, the public seemed to be interested mainly in racing cars, or very large touring cars that only the rich could afford.

Alexander Winton, a Scottish immigrant, who had started out as a bicycle maker, had built a powerful racing car. He had won fame because of his challenge in the summer of 1900 to race a car driven by a Frenchman. Although Winton did not finish the race, his name and his car became known all over the United States. This probably influenced Ford's decision to build a racer, even though he was more interested in designing a car that would have practical use. He thought, too, that if he solved the problem of speed, he could solve the other problems in designing his car.

Again Ford was helped by Ed Huff, who had worked with him in the Edison plant and had helped Ford in designing his first cars. Huff had a fine inventive mind, but he could not be depended upon except in his devotion to Henry Ford. Huff would hold a good job for a month or so, then leave it to try something else. His personal life was also subject to much criticism. In spite of this, Ford was genuinely fond of Huff. He never found fault with him, and frequently got him out of trouble and paid his debts with no questions asked.

Ford had another assistant, C. Harold Wills, a young draftsman. He was a tall, handsome man with a fine personality. He had been trained as a machinist and was anxious to get new experience. The two men worked well together. Wills could understand a design when it was drawn. Ford always had trouble reading blueprints and could comprehend little unless he saw an actual model.

Because Ford could not afford to pay him very

much, Wills worked only part time for Ford and carried another job. However, the part time often extended until the midnight hours.

The racing car that Ford built was huge for the time and a tremendous noise maker. He did not dare drive it through the streets of Detroit. Instead he hired horses to take it out of the city for trials. When Ford drove the racer, Huff knelt on a shelf-like running board. When they came to a curve, Huff hung way out from the handgrips as ballast. He seemed to have neither nerves nor fear.

A race was announced for October 10, 1901, on a mile-long dirt racetrack along the Detroit River in

Henry Ford at the wheel and Ed Huff on the running board of a racing car.

Grosse Pointe. The "Detroit chauffeur, Henry Ford," was one of the contenders. The driver of a car or "chauffeur" was usually the owner. A grand parade of one hundred automobiles moved through the streets of Detroit before the race. Everybody in Detroit seemed to be either watching the parade or at the track. There were about eight thousand people, including Clara Ford and Edsel, in the grandstand or along the track.

The first few events seemed dull, for everyone was eagerly awaiting the final event. It would be a ten-mile race between Alexander Winton and Henry Ford, for all other contenders had withdrawn.

For the first three miles, Winton was in the lead. Then Ford began to catch up, with Ed Huff hanging far out in his efforts to serve as ballast on the curves. On the sixth lap, Ford drew close to Winton. On the eighth lap, he was ahead. With the crowd cheering wildly, for Ford was the underdog, he won the race. He had averaged 1:20⅘ minutes per mile.

The prize was a beautiful cut glass punch bowl set. It had been confidently chosen by Winton's manager, because he thought it would look well in the bay window of the Winton's dining room.

"Well, of all things, to win a cut glass punch bowl," Clara Ford wrote to a friend. "Where will we ever put it?"

By this time the Fords were no longer living with Henry's family but had moved to 332 Hendrie Street,

59

their eleventh rented home. Clara Ford, for one, was happy to be keeping house alone. She finally decided to put the punch bowl on the landing of their new home, though it was much too grand for the modest house in which they were living.

On the day Ford had raced Winton, there had been an earlier race by two famous cyclists, Tom Cooper and Barney Oldfield. Tom Cooper was the best bicycle racer in the country. He was young and well-to-do at the time because he represented bicycle firms for high fees, and he had won many cash prizes. At the racetrack that day, Cooper watched the auto races with increasing interest.

In February, 1902, Cooper came to Detroit and looked up Ford. By this time, Ford had broken all connections with his former backers and was working on his own time and using his own money. Again he was looking for financing in order to continue building racers.

The two men soon had an agreement. Ford would build two racers, one for each of them. Cooper would supply the funds and Ford would do the designing. The two racing cars were called the *999* and the *Arrow*. The *999* was named after a well-known New York Central train that had made a record run from New York to Chicago. The *Arrow* was also named for an express train.

Neither Ford nor Cooper felt able to drive either

car. "Going over Niagara falls would be a pastime for me compared to riding in one of our racers at full speed," said Ford.

Cooper suggested that they engage Barney Oldfield, who also was an outstanding bicycle racer. "There is nothing too fast for him," said Cooper.

Ford telegraphed Oldfield, who was in Salt Lake City at the time, and he came at once to Detroit. He had never driven a motorcar. "But I'll do anything once," he said. Oldfield was a muscular, cheerful-looking man, with a round face, blue eyes, and a composed manner. He seemed perfectly capable of doing what he had said.

The race was to be on October 25, 1902, and was a five-mile event. The week before the race, the *999* was towed at night to Grosse Pointe, for there would

Barney Oldfield behind the wheel of the *999*. Henry Ford standing.

have been a panic in the streets of Detroit if it were driven. "It makes more noise than a freight train," said an observer.

During the week Oldfield practiced driving the car with Huff, who seemingly unafraid, crouched behind the driver. By the end of the week, Oldfield thought he could handle the car well. However, by this time, Ford was afraid that Oldfield would be risking his life and asked him to withdraw.

"Well this chariot may kill me, but they'll say I was going like hell when she took me over the bank," said Oldfield. "I may as well be dead as dead broke," he told a friend, for Oldfield knew that the day of bicycle races was over.

Four drivers, including Oldfield, were entered in the race. Oldfield started off at full speed at once, with nothing but goggles to protect him from dirt and spattering oil. At the end of the first lap he was ahead. For a time, he lost ground, but at the fifth lap he tore ahead and won the race. The time was less than 1:06 minutes per mile, which was an American record. The crowd carried Oldfield around on their shoulders. From that time on, Barney Oldfield was the leading automobile racer in America.

5

The Ford Motor Company

AMONG THE MEN who watched Oldfield win the race
at Grosse Pointe was Alex Y. Malcomson, a prosperous
wood and coal dealer in Detroit. Malcomson was convinced that there was a future in the manufacture of
automobiles. On August 16, 1902, Malcomson with
his lawyer, John W. Anderson, called on Ford. At the
Edison plant, Ford had ordered coal from Malcomson,
and so was acquainted with him. Malcomson now
proposed that they form a company to manufacture
passenger cars of Ford's design.

By this time, Ford had broken off his relations with
Cooper, and so the suggestion appealed to him. He
was no longer interested in building a racer. The
wealthy people who bought cars still wanted only big,
expensive automobiles or racers. But Ford wanted to
build a light, sturdy car that the "workingman could
buy." The roads were terrible outside the cities, and
the small Oldsmobiles and Cadillacs that were being
manufactured were not rugged enough. The big cars,
like the Pierce and Winton, were too high-priced.

The big problem in the beginning was to sell stock in the company. It was difficult to get investors. Malcomson was known to be a speculator. Ford had failed in one business and had withdrawn from another. Men who had money were skeptical because so many manufacturers of cars had failed in business.

James Couzens, Malcomson's bookkeeper, was the chief salesman of the stock. Finally, he induced John S. Gray, a banker and Malcomson's uncle, to invest ten thousand dollars. Albert Strelow, a wealthy builder, invested five thousand dollars and agreed to rent his shop on Mack Street for manufacturing.

John and Horace Dodge each invested five thousand dollars, but they got the contract to manufacture the motors and other parts. However, they were good

Alex Y. Malcomson's coal yard.

businessmen and had the best machine shop in the West. The Dodge brothers were both rough men and heavy drinkers, but excellent mechanics. They were devoted to each other, and from their first working days had refused to take a job unless both were employed. Because they were hardworking and had ability, both rapidly won promotion and in time started their own machine shop and prospered.

On June 16, 1903, the Ford Motor Company was incorporated. There were nine stockholders, in addition to Malcomson, Ford, and Couzens. These nine and Couzens invested $28,000 in cash and pledged $14,000 more in notes. For this, they received forty-nine percent of the stock.

Malcomson and Ford split the remaining fifty-one percent and thus controlled the company. Malcomson had already paid for his share by contributing $7000 to Ford while he worked on his new model. Ford contributed his expert services. Gray was named president; Ford, vice-president and general manager; Malcomson, treasurer; and Couzens, secretary. However, Couzens acted as both treasurer and secretary as Malcomson was occupied with his own coal business.

When Ford and Couzens walked home together the night the company was formed, they talked about the salaries they should expect.

"What do you think we should ask from those fellows?" asked Ford. To him, the only important people in the company were those who would be actually working to produce and sell the cars. The rest of the stockholders were "those fellows."

When the salaries were decided upon, Ford received $3600 a year and Couzens $2500 a year.

On June 16, 1903, the same day on which the company was incorporated, the Ford Motor Company began production. Their plant was the little one-story wagon shop on Mack Street, which Albert Strelow rented to them for seventy-five dollars a month.

Ten workmen were hired, at an average rate of $1.50 a day. All the men worked ten hours a day, but Ford, Couzens, and Wills often worked until midnight and sometimes for all seven days of the week. It was planned to make 650 cars a year, with an output of

Interior of Mack Avenue plant.

fifteen cars a day. "We worked our hearts out to make the fifteen," said a workman, all of whom were eager to be part of the plant.

The first car designed for sale was called Model A. It was comparatively simple, light, and efficient. It had a two-cylinder opposed engine, developed eight horsepower, and could run up to thirty miles an hour. The car had two speeds forward and one reverse. The steering wheel, as in all cars built at this time, was on the right. The wheel base was six feet. The wheels were twenty-eight inches in diameter with wooden spokes.

The men worked on four cars in a group. Once the motor was put together and tested, the car was ready to be assembled. First the wheels were put on, and

The earlier Ford Model A, as restored in Greenfield Village.

then the body. It was so light that two men could lift the body and put it in place. Finally, the fenders were attached. After the car was given a careful test on the streets outside, it was painted. The first cars were brightly colored and looked quite gay.

Ford had said, "I will build a motor car for the multitude . . . so low in price that the man of moderate means may own one and enjoy with his family the blessings of happy hours spent in God's great open spaces." He would have liked to continue with his experiments before the company went into production, but Couzens strongly objected. He refused to permit another change. "Get the money first," he said.

In spite of this, Ford and Couzens worked well together. Ford was in charge of the factory. Couzens did the bookkeeping and advertising. The two men were widely different in personality. Couzens had a violent temper. He kept workers in awe as well as in fear, and he insisted on top performance. Ford also wanted good work, but he got it in a different way. He moved among the men, called them by their first names, and often had a joke or story to tell. "Keep a man cheerful, and he'll work harder," was Ford's philosophy. Many of the men called him Henry.

The first sale of a car was made in the middle of July and just in time. The company had less than three hundred dollars in the bank. The first buyer was a physician in Chicago, Dr. E. Pfenning, for from the beginning, physicians had found it practical to use automobiles. The doctor paid $850 for his car, the full cash price. By the end of July, more than six thousand dollars had been made, and by the end of the year, Couzens had declared more than one hundred thousand dollars in dividends for the stockholders. So the stockholders were able to pay up their notes and never invested more than their original $28,000 in cash.

In that first year, the Ford Motor Company had matters of concern other than financing. In October, shortly after the company was formed, a suit was filed against it by the Association of Licensed Automobile Manufacturers (A.L.A.M.) for infringing on the patent rights of George Baldwin Selden.

George B. Selden, born in 1846, was from a well-to-do family living in Rochester, New York. He attended Yale University, served in the Civil War, studied law, and was admitted to the bar in 1871. Selden, however, was more interested in designing a horseless carriage than in law. He developed a light-weight, three-cylinder engine, which he designed on paper but did not build. He applied for a patent on May 8, 1879, but did not let it be issued. At the time he could not get financial help to manufacture his engine, and he was afraid his patent would expire before he could go into production. He kept his patent from expiring by frequently making small changes in the design and applying for a new patent. In May, 1895, however, he could delay no longer, and the patent was issued.

In 1900, Selden sued the Winton Company, the principal manufacturer at the time, for infringing on his patent rights. As a result, Winton and the other manufacturers of cars formed the Association of Licensed Automobile Manufacturers, and as a group paid royalties to Selden. The Ford Motor Company was not permitted to join the A.L.A.M. because the members did not want any competition.

In July, 1903, before the suit was brought, the A.L.A.M. had advertised, "No other manufacturers are authorized to make or sell gasoline automobiles except the twenty-six firms in the A.L.A.M. . . . Don't

Henry Ford behind wheel, Ed. Huff up front in a racing car.

buy a lawsuit with your car."

In answer to this, the Ford Motor Company, although just making its first sales, advertised, "We will protect you against any prosecution for alleged infringement of patents. . . . We have always been winners." To prove this, the case was in the courts for eight years.

In 1904, the Ford Motor Company offered for sale, Model B, a new and more expensive car selling for $2000. Ford felt that he needed publicity to get the public interested in his new auto. Cars were still being bought chiefly by wealthy people whose main interest was in racing cars. Because of this, Ford offered to break the world speed record in a racer having an engine similar to his new car.

The trial was on January 12, 1904, on Lake St. Clair, just northeast of Detroit. The weather was bitter cold, and Ford had the snow scraped from the ice and the four-mile course covered with cinders. There were official timers to check the run. In spite of the bitter cold, a crowd had turned out to watch, among them Clara and Edsel Ford.

The trial began at two in the afternoon. In the car with Ford was his old reliable friend, Ed Huff, blowing into the tank to keep the gasoline feeding. Ford did make the world's record in the run—39 and $\frac{2}{5}$ seconds for a measured mile, just under the French record; but he never forgot the terror of that run.

"The ice seemed smooth to look at," he said, "but it was full of ruts. Every time the car leaped in the air, I never knew how it would come down. But somehow, I stayed topside up."

But Ford achieved his real objective. The trial put the Ford Model B in the lead, and the Ford cars sold in increasing numbers.

In 1905, the Ford Company moved to a new and larger plant on Piquette Avenue. It was a three-story structure with a large elevator. Owned and built by the company, it was ten times larger than the old plant on Mack Street. "Ford's immense plant," the newspapers called the Piquette Avenue shop.

In that same year, Charles E. Sorenson came to work for Ford. Sorenson was a tall, handsome man of Danish descent. He started in the foundry shop and soon won the confidence of Ford and began to advance. Sorenson's ability to transform his ideas into a model that could be seen and handled pleased Ford, who always had difficulty in reading blueprints. The two men made an excellent team.

Sorenson was a harsh and hard driving man with those who worked under him, but he worked just as hard himself. He had a fierce temper and was hated and feared by the men who called him "Cast Iron Charlie," though they respected him. He was to be part of the Ford organization for forty years.

William S. Knudsen was another Dane who came

to work for Ford in 1912. Like Sorenson, Knudsen was tall and well built. He also had a violent temper, but he controlled it better and had pleasant relationships with the other men. As one Ford worker said, "Sorenson was a wild man, but Knudsen was a mild man." Knudsen's particular ability was in management, and so, in time, he was placed in charge of various plants of the Ford Company. He was an expert in devising short cuts in manufacture.

By 1905, Ford decided to make his own engines and other parts and thus end his dependence on the Dodge brothers. Other automobile companies were

Piquette Avenue plant, Model N in foreground.

following this procedure. Therefore on November 22, 1905, the Ford Manufacturing Company was incorporated. Malcomson was not included among the shareholders. Ford was elected president of the new company with Couzens as treasurer.

Although Malcomson had not taken an active part in the earlier Ford Motor Company because of the demands on his time his own coal business made, he was furious at being excluded. In December, he announced that he was starting a rival company to manufacture cars. He was therefore asked to resign from the Board of the Ford Motor Company since he was acting against the interests of the company. This he finally agreed to do, as he did not want to fight the case in court, and he wanted to develop his own company.

Ford bought Malcomson's shares of stock for $175,000. This was a small amount in relation to the huge profits made by the stockholders later on, but it was a large sum in comparison with the $7000 Malcomson had invested. When John Gray died in 1906, Ford became president of the company. He later bought Gray's stock, as well as the shares of other stockholders as they withdrew from the company. Ford and Couzens now had complete power. Early in 1907, the two Ford companies were combined. It was the largest industry under one roof in Michigan.

Ford continued to be interested in racing, though as a spectator rather than a participant. In 1905, at a racing meet in Palm Beach, Florida, he saw a French car wrecked in a smash-up. Foreign cars, he had noticed, seemed to be stronger than American cars. When he examined the wreck, he picked up a valve stem that was very light and strong.

"This is the kind of material we should have in our cars," Ford said to his associates. "Find out all you can about it."

Ford soon learned that the valve stem was made from a French steel alloyed with vanadium, a new and rare metal. However, no company in America produced this kind of steel. Ford sent for a man in England who knew how to make the steel. Then he founded a small company in Canton, Ohio, which after several trials succeeded in producing the steel. It had three times the strength of the old steel that had been used and was ideal for cars traveling on the poor roads of the United States.

By this time, Ford's relations with the men in the plant had grown more formal. He spent less time now walking about the factory and talking with the men. As the force grew larger, he was no longer able to remember the names of those who were employed, and only the old-timers still called him Henry.

In spite of the big dividends and good salary that Ford received, his family continued to live in a rented home. They had few guests. Usually grape juice was offered for refreshment, for Ford neither

75

Young Edsel Ford (at wheel) pulling sleds with a Model N.

drank nor smoked, and he disliked seeing others do either. The Fords were friendly with the family of James Couzens, though there was a big difference in the ages of their children.

Ford, who was always anxious to improve his car, continually designed new automobiles. Each model was named for a letter of the alphabet, until finally in 1907, Model S was produced. At the Detroit Automobile Show in 1907, Ford talked about something new he had in mind. "It will be like forked lightning," he said. The "something new" was the Model T—the car that would change the whole history of man in this country and bring untold wealth to Henry Ford and his associates.

6

The Model T

By October, 1907, the Ford Motor Company had made models of automobiles from A to S, although not all of these designs were put on the market. The Ford cars were selling for less than $1000. In 1907, the company had its best year and made nearly five million dollars. In the four years since the company had started, about $400,000 had been declared in dividends on a cash investment of $28,000. As a result of the sales, the salaries of the executives were raised continuously until in 1910 both Couzens and Ford received $75,000 a year. The salaries, however, were small in comparison with the handsome dividends and the rise in the value of the stock.

Ford was firmly established now as a manufacturer of automobiles. In addition, he had control of the company, for he had bought the shares of several minor stockholders. In 1907, Ford decided to buy the sixty-acre Highland Park racetrack, which was "way out in the country" then, and to build "the largest automobile factory in the country." The plant was to produce only one type of car—the new Model T.

Ford's principal desire was to design a car that would be light in weight, rugged, easily maintained, and dependable. Then he planned to spend money to produce it efficiently and each year sell it more cheaply. He knew that change in design meant retooling a factory and not studying the design long enough to see how it could be improved. A single, carefully worked out design, made in a plant that was large and efficient, would meet his objectives.

Rival automobile companies were delighted with the news that Ford had bought the Highland Park acreage and planned to build only one type of car. "How soon will Ford blow up?" was the hopeful question asked by his competitors. Other businessmen shook their heads in disbelief. How could anyone build such a huge plant to manufacture only a single type of automobile and that, apparently, for all time?

Nor were all of Ford's associates in the company willing to go along with him in his plan to produce only the Model T in the Highland Park plant and to continue to do that as long as the company would stay in business. Most of them thought the Model T was a good car, but they were opposed to Ford's plan for production.

However, Ford would tolerate no opposition to his ideas. Since he controlled the company, anyone opposed to his program would find himself out of a job.

Sorenson was one man who remained for forty years. He once said, "Mr. Ford never caught me saying that an idea he had couldn't be done. . . . I always felt the thing would prove itself."

It is interesting to note that Henry Ford, who all through the years he had been designing cars had been constantly making changes to improve his machines, now was committed to the idea of making one unchangeable model. But his determination to manufacture the one car that would meet all the qualities he felt should be in an automobile for the general public was stronger than his desire to make changes.

Although Ford had a one-track mind, when it came to the manufacture of his car, he was always open to suggestions for making the design. A dozen men worked with him to develop the Model T. However, Ford should receive most of the credit. He was the one to promote the idea over all opposition, and he gave the greatest number of suggestions for the design. Sorenson was the one who figured out most of the details, but Ford determined quickly whether the method was right or wrong. "Not fast enough," he would say as the experiment was made. "That won't produce enough cars."

The idea for the Model T had started when the Piquette plant had begun to use vanadium steel. Ford had said to Sorenson then, "Charlie, this means an entirely new design for a car. We can make it better, lighter, and cheaper than before." Not long after, he announced that he would build a new experimental room at the plant. "Just for the new car," he said to Sorenson.

Ford's office was on the second floor of the plant. It was simply furnished with straight chairs and a four-by-six-foot flat-topped desk and a rocking chair. There was a big blackboard against the wall. Adjoining the office were a workroom and a toolroom. Ford spent more time in these than in his office.

Often the men worked at night, with Ford sketching his ideas on the blackboard. He would sit in his rocking chair for long periods, studying the sketch and making comments. Usually Ford would have a mock-up made of the car, for he still found it difficult to read blueprints. As a rule, photographs would be taken of the various designs and the miniatures. It was at this time that the Ford Motor Company was being sued for infringing on the patent of an engine designed by George B. Selden, and those working on the design for the Model T may have been conscious of the need to protect their ideas.

As the work progressed, Ford grew more enthusiastic. "Charlie," he said to Sorenson, "we're going to get a car now that we can make in volume and sell at a low price."

The day the first Model T was brought out of the experimental room, Ford was joyfully driven around the streets of Detroit by one of the men who had worked with him on the design. Ford made a point of being driven past the office of Malcomson, for he had always been opposed to manufacturing a low-priced car. In the plant, Ford grinned happily as he slapped his associates on the back. "Well, I guess we've got started," he said again and again.

The Model T was a homely-looking car, but it could take the ruts and holes of the poor roads of the time. It could be easily repaired by a farmhand or anyone with some mechanical skill. Many of the owners, in time, used hay wire, cheap bolts, and even fishhooks to keep the parts together. There were few repairmen in the early days of the automobile, and no garages with standard procedures. The amateur mechanic who could invent the gadgets to keep his Model T functioning properly was the man most delighted with his vehicle.

It is said that the Model T was something like Ford himself. It was tough, simple, and independent, and without show, so that it became the car for the common man. There was no attempt to give a choice of colors with the rush of orders when the car first went into production. At first, the touring cars were painted red, and the roadsters, pearl gray. In time, Ford said that a buyer could have any color "as long as it was black."

Orders for the Model T came in so fast that by May

1, 1909, the whole plant on Piquette Avenue was engaged in making Model T cars and no more orders were taken. Nothing delighted Ford more than to have farmers enthusiastic about his new car. The price of $500 for a runabout and $50 more for a touring car fitted the pocketbooks of the farmers. They were more interested in sound construction than in style. Most of the farmers knew enough about machinery to service their own cars. They not only used their cars for pleasure, but to haul produce and to hitch to attachments for sawing wood or grinding grain. The car was so well built that it lasted for years.

In spite of the ever increasing sales and profits for the Ford Motor Company, and now the prospects for a new model and a new plant, a cloud had hung over the company from its beginning. The suit of the A.L.A.M. against Ford for the infringment of the Selden patents had gone from court to court.

To fight the suit, Ford and Couzens had engaged Ralzemond A. Parker as their attorney. He was not only an eminent lawyer but a specialist in patent law. The A.L.A.M. also engaged outstanding lawyers and submitted over five million words of evidence. As an exhibit, the lawyers brought in the "Selden buggy," a motorcar that had been built by Selden and his sons to show that the machine he had designed would and could run. The vehicle was examined, and several persons rode in it.

It was not until early in 1909 that the Selden case was concluded in the first court. The lawyers from both sides appeared before Judge Hough in New York to get his verdict. Judge Hough knew little about patent law. He tried to be fair in his judgment, but he was more impressed with the arguments of the lawyers for the A.L.A.M. than with the statements of Ford's attorney, Ralzemond Parker.

After careful study, Judge Hough gave his opinion on September 15, 1909. He ruled that all automobile manufacturers were infringing on Selden's patent.

Ford, however, refused to accept this judgment. "We will fight to a finish," he stated. Already he had spent over $200,000. He would continue to fight if necessary, he said, until he was wiped out. The case was taken in November to the Court of Appeals in New York. The Court decided that the manufacturers neither "legally nor morally owed anything to Selden." The Selden car was propelled by an engine of the Otto type. The Ford car and others made in the United States were propelled by an engine of the Brayton type.

To celebrate the victory, the Ford Motor Company gave a banquet about a week later at Rector's, a well-known fashionable restaurant in New York City. Young Edsel Ford probably attended the banquet. He was eighteen years old at the time and attending school. He was a quiet but well-balanced young man, though more interested in motors than in his studies.

The Fords were no longer living in small, rented houses, but had built their own home on a large lot on the corner of Edison and Second Avenue in Detroit. The house was brick, with stone trim and a green tiled roof. The rooms were spacious and the grounds beautiful. Clara engaged a landscape gardener to plan the grounds. A great variety of trees and shrubs were planted. She had a sunken garden, a summer house, and a rose garden.

The Fords had a relatively modest staff of servants now to take care of the house and grounds. Clara had her own electric car to drive around the city. Edsel attended a private school and also had his own car, a Ford Model T. He had driven his first car, a Model A, when he was ten years old.

Each day after school, Edsel rode on his bicycle to the plant and hurried to the experimental room to see what new thing was being tried or planned. Henry Ford was pleased with his son's interest. "I've got a boy I can be proud of," he said.

In the summer of 1912, the Fords sailed for Europe. It was their first trip abroad. They were gone just a little over a month. Ford wanted to see his plants in England and France. While he and Edsel inspected the factories, Clara visited the cathedrals and castles.

Ford was past middle age now. His dark hair was thinner and beginning to show gray. But he was still strong and wiry. A cousin, with the frankness of a relative, wrote of the Fords, "Clara's getting awfully fleshy, and Henry's awfully thin." Clara wasn't really "awfully fleshy," though plumper than when she was as a bride. Ford had always been thin.

The Ford Motor Company had moved to its new plant in Highland Park on January 1, 1910. The building was four stories high, 865 feet long, and 75 feet wide. The building was made of steel and concrete, with wide windows so that there was plenty of light in

Henry, Clara, and Edsel Ford aboard ship en route to Europe.

the plant. Because of its size, all the parts and even the bodies could be made in the plant. Not only was the Highland Park plant well built, but it was said to be the most artistic factory in America at the time. It was clean, shining, and harmonious in design. It was to have the handsomest power plant in the country, with great plate glass windows, so that the machinery and spotless tiled floors could be seen at all times. Henry Ford's mother would have been pleased to see this gleaming plant over which her son presided.

The movement from the Piquette plant to Highland Park was made with no formal ceremony. No speeches were made, no brass band played, there was no ribbon cutting. On the last day of 1909, the Model T Fords rolled out of the Piquette plant. On the following day, they were moving out from Highland Park. Only one-fourth of the building was completed by this time, but through the years, department after department was added until the whole structure was completed.

7

Mass production

HENRY FORD HAD ALWAYS had a keen desire to simplify operations and to save time and material in the manufacture of his cars. With Sorenson, he experimented with a crude assembly line at the Piquette plant during the last year of occupancy. A line about thirty or forty feet long was built of railroad ties. A chassis was put on the rails and pulled forward with a rope. Then the front and rear axles were slid along at a rate that permitted the workmen to connect all the parts as the chassis moved forward.

Mass production and a form of assembly line methods had already begun in the manufacture of other products. Parts were standardized and therefore interchangeable in firearms, sewing machines, bicycles, and some farm machinery. They were being manufactured so that each worker did only a certain part of the whole procedure. In this way, time and labor were saved. But Ford's experiments at the Piquette plant were the first attempt by the automotive industry to use this method of production.

However, there was no real effort to develop an assembly plant made by the Ford Motor Company until after the Highland Park plant had been in operation about two years. Then, conveyor belts were installed that took parts to assemblers and passed them on to the next group of workers. Sorenson and Ford were chiefly responsible for the development. They got their idea for the conveyor belts from the trolley lines used by the Chicago meat-packers.

Before the development of the assembly line, the car had remained stationary while workers went to places in the shop to get parts to attach to the machine. Now the work was brought to the men at a waist-high level. No worker had to stoop to attach a bolt or screw.

Assembling magnetos on a conveyor belt, about 1913.

Everything traveled on a moving platform. Nothing was lifted or trucked. Each team of men did a little work, and then the frame moved on to the next team.

It took several years to get the whole procedure to work out smoothly; once it functioned satisfactorily, there were few changes as long as the Model T was being produced. Each portion of the work was so uniform and simple that unskilled laborers could be trained to handle a specific job in a short time. The Ford Motor Company had no use for experience anymore. It wanted men who would simply do as they were told, over and over again from bell time to bell time.

The treatment of workers from this time on became increasingly harsh, even though the rules, in many cases, were necessary. Absolute silence was required because concentration was needed. Smoking was strictly forbidden. There was an attempt even to stop the chewing of tobacco. However, when it was learned that men got sick because they swallowed the tobacco if they thought they would be caught, they were provided with paper spittoons. To enforce the rules, "spotters" moved about among the men and made reports.

There was a ten-hour day for the force, and a lunch period of fifteen minutes. This included the time to wash up. A lunch wagon came around to the shop. For fifteen cents, a man could buy a substantial sandwich, a piece of cake or pie, and coffee or milk.

The production goal was always being raised and men made to work harder and faster. "Ford was one of the worst shops for driving men," said William C. Klann, an executive, who had been dismissed on short notice.

The principal grievance, however, was not haste or pressure but the uncertainty of holding a job. Dismissals were abrupt and often the result of the whim of a foreman. Nor was promotion made on the basis of seniority. By this procedure, poor workers could be eliminated. The employees were not permitted to form a union to get redress for their grievances, though union men were hired. Nor was there any kind of incentive pay for suggestions to improve production.

However, most of these practices were found in all the automotive industries. William S. Knudsen, who had worked for Ford and then for General Motors, boasted that he had learned to shout, "Hurry up!" in fifteen different languages. He did this when later he was in charge of the Chevrolet Division of General Motors as well as at Ford's. There were objections to the work on the assembly lines not because the tasks were difficult but because of the effect of the constant repetition of the task on the man himself. Sociologists were shocked by the monotony of the work and wrote and spoke against it. In time, however, other automotive companies, and eventually all industries, adopted the assembly line procedure.

A study made by a Yale Research group stated that unless a man was unusually nervous or slow, he should have no difficulty working on an assembly line. It was found, too, that men who had done manual work outdoors, and in all kinds of weather, found working in a plant on an assembly line a far easier job.

The Model T was usually called the "Tin Lizzy," especially by the college boys, or the "Flivver." But there were other names which indicated its character. "Leaping Lena," or "Bouncing Betty," or "Galloping Snail" were familiar. The names were given in fond derision, and many a farmer had his own pet name for his favorite and highly prized vehicle.

Stories and jokes were told. Books were published containing most of them. "Henry can make them faster than we can wreck them," was stated. "If we had milk and sugar, this would be a milk shake," was another. A farmer asked that his grave be made large so that his Ford could be buried with him because it had gotten him out of so many holes.

Ford did nothing to stop the ridicule. He knew the humor was kindly and was good publicity. "A story on the front page is more valuable than advertising," he said.

It was at this time that Ford's friendship with Harvey S. Firestone and John Burroughs began. Ford bought most of his tires from Firestone, who had been manufacturing them in Akron, Ohio, since 1900. Ford

John Burroughs cranking his Model T.

had known Firestone in Detroit, where he sold buggies before moving to Chicago and then to Ohio. The business relationship between the two men developed into a close friendship. Firestone pioneered the pneumatic tires for the Model T.

Ford had always taken a deep interest in wild life, especially birds. Because of this he read the books and essays on birds and flowers written by the naturalist, John Burroughs. In 1912, Ford wrote to Burroughs and told him of his interest in wild life. He offered to send Burroughs a Model T car and a man to teach him how to drive. In June, Burroughs came to Detroit to visit Ford, and their friendship grew from that time. Burroughs thought Ford a "lovable man."

8

The five-dollar day

By 1913, Detroit was becoming the center of the automotive industry. Its location provided good land and water transportation. There were hundreds of machine shops and factories already established to manufacture carriages, wagons, freight cars, and Pullman cars. Three of the prominent manufacturers of automobiles, through circumstances rather than plan, had begun their manufacturing in Detroit. They were Henry Ford, Ransom E. Olds, and Henry Leland.

In the beginning of the twentieth century, Detroit had an abundant supply of labor. The many industries in the city attracted large numbers of immigrants from Europe. However, by 1910, as the automotive industry developed, the demands for labor often exceeded the supply. Manufacturers in other industries complained because the men preferred to work in the automotive plants. The workers not only received better pay and had a chance for promotion, but they were attracted by a new and progressive industry.

Until 1910, the Ford Motor Company had little difficulty in obtaining workers. As yet, it was one of the smaller companies. The workmen were also interested in being part of the development of the Model T car. The Ford company had a better record for safety precautions and warning devices than any other automotive company. Its standard of wages was as high as in other industries. Its Highland Park plant was the finest and cleanest in which to work. In addition, Ford had a modest profit-sharing plan, and workers were given a bonus at the end of each year.

However, like all manufacturers in Detroit, the Ford Company was plagued with the problem of turnover in labor as men quit their jobs for others that offered them higher wages or better working conditions.

By 1913, the Ford Motor Company had paid out more than fifteen million dollars in dividends to its stockholders on an original cash investment of $28,-000. In addition, the company paid enormous salaries to its executives. It had a huge surplus set aside for expansion, and each year it had lowered the price of its cars. In a newspaper interview, Ford said that the profits of his company were "awful." The stockholders, executives, and customers had benefitted. Only the workers had not shared in the profits. The wage rate at Ford's at the time was twenty-six cents an hour for unskilled labor, and fifty-four cents for skilled workers. This was the average pay in industry. The working day was nine hours.

From incidents of fighting that Ford had observed in his plant, he was of the opinion that the workers were dissatisfied because they were paid only enough for a bare subsistence. On December 31, 1913, there was a meeting of the directors of the Ford Company in Ford's office at the Highland Park plant. It was larger than his Piquette office and handsomely furnished, but, as usual, Ford spent more time in the plant than in his office. A large blackboard on one wall was still a standard piece of equipment.

With Ford at the meeting were James Couzens, Charles Sorenson, C. Harold Wills, and other executives. They planned to discuss the bonus for the year as well as a general wage raise for workers in the plant.

Ford covered the blackboard in his office with the figures for the income made, the dividends paid out,

James Couzens (left) and Henry Ford, about 1914.

the salaries paid to executives, and the wages of the workers. The total paid out in wages was very small in comparison with the dividends and the salaries of the executives.

"The wages we pay are too small in comparison with our profits," said Ford. "I think we should raise our minimum daily pay rate."

He wrote $3.00 on the blackboard and studied it for a minute. Then he wrote $3.50 and after this $3.75. Then more rapidly he wrote $4.00; then $4.50; and finally $4.75.

There was argument then among the directors, though most of them supported Ford's idea. Couzens, however, was horrified. "Well, it's up to $4.75," he snarled, "why don't you make it $5.00 a day."

"I will," said Ford, and he wrote $5.00 on the blackboard.

A second directors' meeting was held on January 5, 1914. The figures were reviewed and the wage scale and other points determined. By this time, Couzens approved of the program. As a matter of fact, he claimed in later years that he had originated the idea.

The program for a minimum five-dollar-a-day wage at the Ford plant was announced to the newspapers on the day of the second meeting. It was to go into effect on Monday, January 12. Every workman who was twenty-two years old or over would receive "a share in the profits of the house," so that the minimum

$10,000,000 TO 25,000 EMPLOYES OF FORD COMPANY

Head of Motor Company Announces Scheme of Profit Sharing with Workmen.

DAY REDUCED FROM NINE TO EIGHT HOURS

All Over Twenty-Two Years Old To Be Beneficiaries, Except Women and Children.

Commonest Laborer to Get $5 a Day

[SPECIAL DESPATCH TO THE HERALD.]
DETROIT, Mich., Monday.—"The commonest laborer who sweeps the floors of the factory shall receive his $5 per day. We believe in making 25,000 men prosperous and contented rather than follow the plan of making a few slave drivers in our establishment multi-millionaires.

"(Signed) HENRY FORD."

[SPECIAL DESPATCH TO THE HERALD.]
DETROIT, Mich., Monday.—An epoch in the world's industrial history was marked in Detroit to-day.

A few typewritten lines given out by Henry Ford, head of the Ford Motor Company, bore in concrete fashion the story. By its wording twenty-five thousand men in the army of Detroit's laborers at forge and stamp, at drill and press will be lifted from the position of wage earners to that of sharers in profits of the company, and $10,000,000—about half of the earnings of the great concern—will flow into their pockets in the next year.

This means that every man of the vast Ford organization will find his income increased greatly, in some cases more than one hundred per cent. The man who sweeps the floor will receive not less than $5 a day, and as each round in the ladder of industry is reached the

HENRY FORD

men on that round will have their salaries added to in proportion.

In addition to this sweeping stride toward a more equal distribution of profits between capital and labor the hours of the employes will be cut from nine to eight per day.

Reproduction of newspaper article announcing the eight-hour, five-dollar day at the Ford plant.

wage would be five dollars a day. Young men under twenty-two would share if they had dependents. Women also would get a raise in pay. The foreign plants of the Ford Motor Company would be asked to increase their wage scale. In this way, nine-tenths of the workers would get the advance at once. In addition, there were to be three shifts of eight hours each. A ten-hour-plus day was the usual practice until Ford's eight-hour day was inaugurated.

"This," said Ford to reporters, "is neither charity nor wages, but profit sharing and efficient engineering."

The public in general approved of the plan, but there was some criticism. Rival companies, especially, stated that Ford was doing this in order to get the pick of the labor force. But as Ford hired unskilled workers and had them trained on the spot, this did not apply. In time, all the automotive industries had to adopt the same wage scale and hours.

"I expect to get more efficient labor because living standards will be raised, and the men will be satisfied to work," Ford said in reply to the criticism.

There has been much discussion as to why Ford started this program. The five dollars a day as a minimum wage was almost double the pay of those lowest on the wage scale, and to make this the standard was like a revolution. But Ford always liked to do something that was dramatic, and the very suddenness of the announcement was spectacular.

Although Ford was personally shy in public, he liked publicity. He considered it good advertising for his car. He wanted to be considered the friend of labor. Most probably he thought that he could get more work out of his men if he paid them more than the current scale. In addition, a higher wage scale, which in time would spread to all industries, would make it possible for families to buy automobiles, and why not the Model T; since that was the car especially designed for the working man.

The five-dollar-day wage scale was the most advanced labor policy in the world. Ford had thought it would cost his company about ten million dollars a year. However, because of increased production, the cost was a little over five million dollars. About eight years later, Ford introduced the five-day week. "Every man needs more than one day for rest and recreation," he said.

There was a depression in the United States in 1914 and much unemployment in Detroit. By two o'clock in the morning on the day after the announcement had appeared in the newspapers, thousands of workers began to gather around the Highland Park plant. By the middle of the morning, the "No Hiring" sign went up on the gates. In spite of the sign, crowds milled around the plant all day and the police had trouble keeping order. In addition, during the week, fourteen thousand letters of application for jobs were received. Many men from other towns used their last cent to pay for the cost of their transportation and for lodging in Detroit.

By Saturday, the sign on the gate stated that all hiring had ceased. In spite of this, on Monday, January 12, the date when the program was to go into effect, about ten thousand men were crowded around the plant by seven-thirty in the morning. When the gates were not opened for them, the men began to boo and yell. They surged against the gates and fought with the guards, who tried to hold the crowd back. Then the men tried to break down the doors of the plant.

By this time, the police had arrived and at once turned fire hoses on the crowd. It was bitter cold. The temperature was nine below zero, and the men were drenched with icy water. They quickly dispersed, though throwing stones at the building as they left. By the end of the day, a new rule was announced by the Ford company. No one would be hired unless he had lived in Detroit for at least six months.

One of the rules for employment under the new scale was that men who were under twenty-two years of age must be, "sober, saving, steady, and industrious," to get the minimum wage. This was a time of high immigration. The foreigners usually lived in nationality islands and under very bad conditions. Some of these conditions were of their own making.

Many of them were planning to work in the United States only long enough to earn sufficient money to permit them to return to the country of their birth and live there more comfortably than they had previously.

To make this money, not only both parents but all of the children of working age were employed. The families lived in crowded tenements, and even took boarders to increase their income. Because of these conditions, Ford created a Sociological Department for his plant. In his opinion, the five-dollar day would give the workers a wide margin over their subsistence, and they would need guidance to spend this money properly.

The Sociological Department was under the direction, in the beginning, of a sociologist, John R. Lee. He was a man with a warm heart and a desire to improve the living conditions of working people.

Three months after the announcement of the five-dollar-a-day program, Ford said to Lee, "I want to see every family have a comfortable home with a bath and a little garden. And I want every employee of mine owning an automobile."

"A Ford automobile?" asked Lee, probably smiling to himself.

"Well, that might be going too far," answered Ford, though in all probability, he thought the Model T was the best automobile his employees could buy.

Lee and his assistants each had the use of a car

and an interpreter to talk to the families. They checked the conditions of the homes, their ownership, the amount of money saved, the recreation of the family, and so on. In time, Lee had about one-hundred and fifty people on his staff. At that time, he was succeeded by Reverend Samuel S. Marquis, who had worked with Lee as a volunteer.

The new director of the Sociological Department was the rector of St. Paul's Cathedral in Detroit, the Episcopalian church attended by the Fords. He was forty-two years old at the time, and had a cheerful temper, a great deal of energy, and a keen interest in the life of the working man.

In 1916, his doctor ordered Reverend Marquis to take a year's leave of absence from his church work. He decided instead to try a change of occupation. He willingly accepted Ford's offer to head the Sociological Department as the successor to John R. Lee. The Fords knew Reverend Marquis intimately and called him "Mark." He was especially liked by Mrs. Ford.

The task of the Sociological Department was difficult both under Lee and Marquis. Some of the workers did not object to their slum conditions. They had known little better before they had come to the United States. They were accustomed now to the grime and close quarters in which they were living. They liked the neighborliness of tenement life and were not concerned about their lack of privacy. They seemed afraid of grass and gardens.

Most of all, they resented having their personal life pried into by outsiders. Many of those on the staff of the Sociological Department, though well meaning, were too inquisitive and were tactless in the way they handled the people whom they queried.

Most of the families, however, did learn to live in a better way. Ford wanted the wives of his men to be good housekeepers, to educate their children, and to buy properly. The families were encouraged to save and to budget their expenses. The women were taught to market properly. They were given instruction in household management and in hygiene. Because of the emphasis on soberness, drinking declined sharply among the men.

The best results were in education. Ford wanted those among his employees who were immigrants to become citizens, and a knowledge of English was required for this. In addition, he wanted them to be able to read the instructions at the plant. An English school was started in May, 1914, which all immigrant employees had to attend. A full course of seventy-two lessons was needed for a diploma.

A trade school was also started for all boys who wanted a technical education. In the trade school, the boys spent one third of their time in school and the rest at work. They received a small salary and had three weeks vacation in the summer and one week at Christ-

English class for foreign-born employees in session on the grounds of a Ford plant.

mas. Most of the courses were technical. There was very little academic work. There was always a waiting list of students, and a boy was assured of a job after graduation even in the Depression. No trade school boy ever had trouble getting a job in any of the automotive plants.

The treatment of Negroes in the Ford plant was progressive. William Perry, an old friend of Henry Ford with whom he had worked in his farming days, was the first Negro hired in 1914. The number grew until Negroes made up one tenth of the working force. "Races should labor as partners," said Ford. "Merit not color should govern promotion."

Ford was also the first one in the automotive industry to hire handicapped people. "It is wrong to put an able-bodied man in a job that can be filled by a cripple. . . . It is a waste to put the blind at weaving baskets," said Henry Ford.

It was said that Ford hired the handicapped for publicity. However, whether this is true or not, his doing so made it a practice that other industries followed.

Henry Ford was opposed to giving charity to anyone. He wanted to help people personally by providing better jobs with good pay, and by seeing that his employees had good homes.

However, on October 1, 1915, the Ford Hospital was opened. Here fees were moderate, the equipment was the best, and all rooms had private baths. The hospital was well staffed with physicians, who received good pay but were not permitted to have any outside practice.

During the war, the Ford Hospital was taken over by the government. It was reopened as a private institution on November 10, 1919, and the same high standards were maintained.

By 1914, there were seven thousand dealers in the United States who were selling Ford cars. They were chosen with care. They were men of good standing in their community and financially responsible. In addition, there were thirty branch agencies and service stations. Nine more were in Canada; three in Europe; and one each in Australia and South America. No other car had such worldwide use. In countries where little English was spoken, almost everyone understood the meaning of the word *Ford*.

Ford believed in giving service for his cars. Many of the dealers had sold bicycles or other vehicles in the past, but they knew little about automobiles. Ford sent out mechanics to instruct the dealers, for he wanted them to be able to give service on the cars they sold. This was important, for there were few mechanics who could repair a car and no garages doing this type of work.

9

Crusade for peace

ON JUNE 28, 1914, Archduke Francis Ferdinand of Austria, the heir to the throne of the Austrian Empire, and his wife were assassinated in Bosnia, an Austrian province. The assassins were members of a secret Serbian organization.

About a month after the assassination, Austria declared war on Serbia. In less than two weeks, because of secret alliances, Germany joined with Austria, and later, Turkey and Bulgaria were united with them. They were known as the Central Powers. Russia, France, England, and later Italy—the Allies—came to the aid of Serbia. The war spread to the colonial possessions of these powers, and to smaller countries; and thus World War I began.

At first the United States was completely neutral, and there was no thought that this country would become involved. Sentiment among the people was divided, and there was open support of one side or the other by various groups. As time went on, we became more sympathetic toward the Allies, mainly because a large portion of our population was of English ancestry, and we read and heard more English propaganda.

Woodrow Wilson, a Democrat, the President at the time, was a pacifist, and tried to maintain our neutrality. We sold to both sides, but as England at first controlled the seas, we sold more to the Allies. Later German submarine warfare hampered this trade and in time brought the United States into the war.

Henry Ford was strongly opposed to war, especially if it involved the United States. Although Ford was a nominal Republican, he supported President Wilson because of his efforts to maintain the neutrality of the United States. Ford's support of Wilson was especially important in 1916 when Wilson ran for a second term with the slogan, "He kept us out of war." Wilson won in this election but by a very close vote.

Ford was among the leaders who were working to bring the conflict in Europe to an end. In the fall of 1915, two of the leaders in the peace movement had an interview with Ford at his home. One was Rosika Schwimmer, a noted Hungarian writer and lecturer. The other was Louis P. Lochner, a leader in the student movement for world peace. Both felt that if President Wilson called a meeting of delegates from neutral nations, the war might come to an end.

Ford had said openly, "If I can be of any service to end this war, and keep America out of it, I shall do it if it costs every dollar and friend that I have."

The two leaders in their interview reminded Ford of this statement. "What do you want me to do?" he asked them.

They suggested that he first call a meeting in New York of all persons in the United States who were interested in the peace movement.

Ford was enthusiastic about the suggestion. "Men sitting around a table, and not dying in the trenches will settle the differences," he said.

The meeting was called, and it was suggested that a commission be sent to Europe.

"Why not have the delegates go in a special ship?" Lochner proposed, though partly in jest.

Ford agreed immediately to the proposal. By evening, the *Oscar II,* a Scandinavian-American liner, was chartered. Ford promised to pay all the expenses.

Ford's next step was to go to Washington to have an interview with President Wilson. Ford wanted the President to be the one to appoint the commission, and thus it would have more recognition. The President was pleasant to Ford in the interview, but he refused to make the appointment. He wanted time to study other plans, he said.

"If you feel you can't act, I will," said Ford. He did not have a high regard for the President as a result of the interview. The President, thought Ford, after his talk, was a "small man." Ford did not realize that the

President as head of state had to act with much more thought and study than one of its leading citizens.

At a press conference in New York, Ford told reporters of his plan to have people interested in a program for peace go to Europe on a privately chartered ship. The story got full publicity, but from the beginning the idea was ridiculed in the newspapers. The derision continued as the days passed and the program progressed.

Over one hundred invitations were telegraphed to people who had expressed interest and were leaders in the desire for peace. Among them were Thomas Edison, William Jennings Bryan, Jane Addams, and John Burroughs. Many, for various reasons, most of which were truthful, did not accept the invitation, though a number expressed their approval of the plans. However, there was still a large number who agreed to go, though only nine days had been spent in preparation. Mrs. Ford was opposed to the idea, not because she was against a peace program, but because of the unfavorable publicity to which her husband was being subjected. She persuaded Reverend Marquis, though he was strongly opposed to the idea, to go with the group and protect her husband from insult as much as he could.

The ship sailed on December 4, 1915. It was a cold, rainy day, but fifteen thousand people were at the Hoboken Dock to see the *Oscar II* depart. Many were well-wishers, but others were there to scoff and laugh. Thomas Edison and his wife were with Mrs. Ford and Edsel on board ship before the leave-taking.

At three o'clock, the *Oscar II* moved slowly out of the harbor, with Henry Ford standing at the rail waving quite seriously to the crowd and throwing them American Beauty roses. On the dock stood Mrs. Ford and Edsel, their faces washed with tears as the ship moved slowly out of sight.

Throughout the journey, the reporters and cartoonists sent material filled with ridicule to their newspapers. When it was suggested to Ford that he refuse to send the stories by wireless from the ship, he said, "The reporters are my guests. I wouldn't for the world censor them."

The *Oscar II* sailing for Europe.

On a stormy day, shortly before the *Oscar II* reached Great Britain, Ford was drenched by a giant wave as he walked on deck. As a result, he contracted a very bad cold. At four o'clock in the morning on December 18, the ship docked at Oslo, Norway. It was twelve below zero that morning, and the welcoming committee was disappointed that Ford was not able to receive them because of his bad cold. Partly because of this, the program got little support in Norway.

Ford's health did not improve, and finally he told Lochner, "I guess I had better go home to mother.

Reverend Samuel Marquis (left) and Henry Ford on board the *Oscar II.*

You've got this thing started now, and can get along without me."

On December 23, 1915, Ford left Oslo for the United States on a regular passenger ship. Reverend Marquis went with him. Although the party was depressed by Ford's personal withdrawal from the program, the *Oscar II* continued on to Sweden, where the reception was cordial. With the permission of the Germans, the party then went by train to The Hague, the seat of government of the Netherlands. Here the delegates for a neutral conference were chosen, and then the members of the party returned to the United States by other ships.

In spite of the scoffing by the newspapers, the delegates continued their efforts for peace until the United States declared war on April 7, 1917. A large number of Americans, even then, respected Ford's idealism. Today the ridicule of the program by the press is considered shameful.

On the twenty-fifth anniversary of the sailing of the *Oscar II*, the editor of *The Detroit Free Press* wrote, "We do not laugh any more, nor joke, when that unique argosy is mentioned. We mourn rather the disappearance of times when men could still believe that even those in the throes of blood lust might be led to reason. No peace ship has sailed since the Second World War began. It could find no port either geographically or in the hearts of men."

Ford himself never did admit that his idea for a peace ship was a mistake, although he did realize that the project had been planned and executed too hastily. Several years after his death, the Peace Flag that had been especially designed and flew at the masthead of the *Oscar II* was found among his treasures.

In 1917, Henry Ford made a complete and rapid change in his opinions and statements regarding the participation of the United States in the war. Early in the year, he was still bitterly and openly opposed to "preparedness" for fear that the program would bring about involvement. But when, on February 3, 1917, President Wilson severed diplomatic relations with Germany, Ford, though somewhat reluctantly, stated, "Well, we must stand behind the President."

Two days later, Ford seemed more resigned. "I cannot believe that war will come," he stated, "but in the event of a declaration of war I will place our factory at the disposal of the United States government and will operate without one cent of profit."

Ford made this statement almost independently, not only because he was the chief stockholder in the company, but because there was no one else in a strong enough position to determine the policies of the company.

Ford and Couzens had gradually drawn apart even before the war in Europe started. Ford's chief interest was in improving the design and manufacture of his car. He was indifferent toward anything that had to do with the business operation of the plant, which was mainly under Couzens. Ford appreciated Couzens' ability but was irritated by his domineering manner. Ford was displeased, too, because Couzens gradually seemed to be more interested in a political career than in the Ford plant.

By 1915, the two men differed widely in their attitudes toward the war being waged in Europe. Couzens, who was Canadian born, was in favor of helping the Allies. He wanted Ford to manufacture munitions for England. Ford, who at this time was violently opposed to war said, "I would rather burn down my factory than supply materials for war."

When Ford expressed his pacifist views in material that he wanted used in advertisements for the Ford Company, Couzens, who was in charge of advertising, refused to let it be printed.

"It's going to stay in," said Ford.

"Then I'm through," said Couzens.

Ford hesitated for a moment. After all, he and Couzens had worked together since the beginning of the company. Then he said, "Well, all right."

On October 12, 1915, Couzens resigned as vice-president of the company, though he still continued as one of the directors.

Henry Ford contributed more to the war effort than any of the manufacturers of automobiles. He had a fine working force and a well-organized plant at Highland Park. He was to expand his plant considerably before the war was over.

In 1915, Ford began buying land along the River Rouge. Highland Park could not be expanded, and Ford felt he needed more land near water power and transportation. At first he said he wanted to build a plant to smelt iron and make coke.

The site selected did not seem a good one for a large plant. It was three miles west of Detroit. Most of the transportation of the time was by railroad rather than water. But the war contributed to the growth of the River Rouge plant. By 1925, ore carriers from the Great Lakes were bringing ore to the docks. Steamers from Europe now had a port, and all supplies needed by Ford could be transported by water. Long docks, railroad yards, blast furnaces, coke ovens, and a thirty-acre foundry were part of the plant. The foundry was said to be the largest in the world.

World War I ambulances ready to be shipped from the Highland Park plant.

Ford's first war contract was for ambulances, the next for helmets. He felt he could do the best with quantity production of airplanes. The Liberty Motor for airplanes had been designed in the United States. Ford was asked in June, 1917, to make engines for the planes.

In the summer of 1917, Ford conferred with Edward R. Hurley, the Chairman of the United States Shipping Board. As a result, Ford began building a new type of ship to hunt down submarines. They were

117

called "Eagle Boats," and were built in quantity at the River Rouge plant. Ford's final effort was to build tanks.

An unhappy effect of the war for Henry Ford was caused by the attacks on his son Edsel for not being in military service. Edsel had been exempted because he was "indispensable to the war industry." Ford insisted that he was responsible for keeping Edsel out of service. "He has wanted to go since the day we declared war," said Ford. "When it is stated by those in authority that Edsel is needed more in the army than in our plant, he will be found at the front and not at a mahogany desk in the war office."

When war had been declared, Ford had promised that he would operate "without one cent of profit." But it was difficult to estimate how much was actual profit for him from the war contracts he received. In the end, because of taxes and the losses due to the sudden ending of the war, his real profits were said to be less than a million dollars.

Ford never returned even this much to the government, though the amount would have been small for him. He was criticized for this; but his impatient nature, the long delay, and the arguments over the money he had made probably made him give up the idea of returning his profits. In reality, it is thought that he actually lost twenty to forty times the amount because of the changes in his industry.

10

A family company and politics

HENRY FORD HAD BECOME a legend in the United States by the end of World War I. Every move he made or opinion he expressed was publicized. "What is Henry doing now?" was the question asked, and everybody knew which "Henry" was meant.

There were changes in the personal life of the Fords even before the United States declared war. Since 1907, they had lived in the big, brick house on Edison Avenue. But as Ford grew rich and famous, swarms of uninvited guests and gawking tourists invaded the grounds and came to the door of his home. Finally, he had to have a guard at the door to keep out the unwelcome throng.

"If we could build the house we want, I'd like it to be near Dearborn," said Clara, with fond memories of her girlhood and early married life.

The Fords had begun buying land near the Rouge River in 1908. Ford liked birds and had put up bird-houses and laid out feeding grounds for a bird sanctuary. In time, the Fords owned 3700 acres along the river and decided to build their home there. "We like country life," said Henry Ford. The site of his new home was about a mile from the house in which he had been born, and about five miles from the River Rouge plant. Dearborn was about twenty miles away. The Fords planned to call their house Fair Lane, after the area in Ireland from which the Ford family had migrated.

Work was begun on Fair Lane in 1913. The estate already had a six room house in which the Fords had lived during previous weekends. In 1915, they moved into a two-story house near the present gatehouse, where they lived while Fair Lane was being built. It was completed by December, 1915. Two different architects worked on the house, for the Fords wanted it built according to their own ideas. The house was built on a bend in the River Rouge and surrounded by woodland. It was a plain structure of no particular style of architecture, built like a fortress, of gray Kelly Island limestone. It had a large swimming pool and bowling alley, and its own power plant on the River Rouge. In all, including the gardens, it cost about two million dollars.

Most of the rooms were panelled in dark, rich woods, with sterling silver lighting fixtures and hardware. A wide panelled hall with a richly carved wooden staircase gave entrance to the rooms. A long driveway, carefully screened by guards and a lodge house, led

Aerial view of Fair Lane. House on left, power plant, right, the River Rouge in the foreground.

from the imposing iron gates to the main house. The entire property was fenced. "I like privacy in my home. Without this protection, my place would become a public park overrun by strangers," said Ford.

There was an artificial lake and several pools on the estate. Near the house, toward the south and east, stretched the gardens, which were Clara's chief delight. There were six different types of gardens, carefully laid out by landscape gardeners, but supervised by Clara. Her greatest pride was the three-acre rose garden, in which all varieties of roses were planted so that they were in bloom throughout the season.

Ford enjoyed the wilder aspects of his grounds. He liked to take long walks, to leap over fences and hedges, and to skate in the wintertime. He loved the trees and never cut one down if it was possible to save it. He spent hours watching the bird life on the grounds and had five-hundred birdhouses, or "hotels" as he called them. In the winter, a big basin of water for the birds was kept from freezing by an electric heater. Baskets filled with suet and other food for the birds were hung from the trees.

The Fords lived simply at Fair Lane. "I like to eat potatoes with their jackets on," said Ford, "and I don't want a man standing at my back and laughing to himself while I eat them." When alone or with the family, the Fords ate at a small table in an alcove of the big, handsome dining room. From here, they could watch the winding River Rouge and the spacious, landscaped grounds. Sometimes, it is said, Ford had a snack in the kitchen.

Many distinguished guests came to Fair Lane. There was an "Edison Room," set aside for Ford's favorite guest. The house was well staffed, and the Fords were gracious hosts, but there was no elaborate entertaining of their guests. The Fords had little social life otherwise, and they took no part in the affairs of the community in which they lived.

On November 1, 1916, Edsel Ford was married to Eleanor Lowthian Clay. Her mother, Mrs. William

Clay, was the sister of J. L. Hudson, the founder of Detroit's largest department store. The Clays and Hudsons lived on Boston Boulevard East and were socially prominent as well as wealthy. The Fords had lived on Edison Avenue, not far from the Clays. The two young people had known each other since they were teenagers. Edsel liked golf, popular music, yachting, and dancing and so had shared the interests and social life of Eleanor. The wedding reception was in the home of the Clays.

Among the guests at the wedding reception were John and Horace Dodge. There was nothing in their conduct that evening to indicate anything but friendly relations with Henry Ford. On the following day, November 2, 1916, the brothers filed a suit in the State Circuit Court of Michigan against the Ford Motor Company. They wanted to halt the expansion of the River Rouge plant and to compel the company to distribute seventy-five percent of the cash surplus in dividends to the stockholders. On the same day, the Circuit Court issued a restraining order against further expansion of the Rouge plant.

The Dodge suit was in court until February, 1919. Then the Supreme Court of Michigan ruled that the Ford Company had to pay the stockholders a little over $19,000,000 from the surplus profits, plus interest at five percent from the date of the first court decision.

"If you want to carry out things to extremes you

should buy out the other stockholders," the Dodge brothers told Ford.

They were willing to sell their own stock, even though they would lose their big dividends from the Ford Company, because they had begun manufacturing their own cars and needed money for expansion.

After the Dodge suit, Henry Ford was determined to get full control of his company so that his decisions could no longer be criticized by any of the other stockholders. However, if he attempted to buy up their stock outright, he would have to pay a high price, for the Ford Company was making more than sixty million dollars a year. He, therefore, resorted to a not uncommon business practice.

In December, 1918, he resigned as president of the company, with his son Edsel to succeed him in that office. The following March, the newspapers announced that Henry Ford planned to start a new company to manufacture a car that would be cheaper than the Model T. The new company was to be owned entirely by the members of the Ford family.

There was panic now among the Ford dealers as well as the other Ford Company stockholders, although Edsel Ford assured them that the new car would not be ready for two or three years. Secret agents then went to the other stockholders and bought up their shares. Only James Couzens, at that time, refused to sell. He was certain that Henry Ford was behind the purchases being made, and he raised the price of his stock to one thousand dollars a share.

The sale of stock was completed by July 11, 1919. The Ford Company was now one big unit owned entirely by one family. Henry Ford had no compunction about the way in which he had secured control. The success of the company had been largely due to his efforts. In the sale of the stock, all of the original stockholders had received many times the amount of their original small investment. Couzens' sister Rosetta, for instance, who was a schoolteacher, had been persuaded by him to invest one hundred dollars of her savings. For this, she received $355,000, in addition to large dividends through the years.

Couzens himself got more than twenty-nine million dollars for his cash investment of twenty-five hundred dollars. In addition, he had had a large salary, and his share of the thirty million dollars in dividends paid to the stockholders since the company had started.

While the Dodge suit and the purchase of stock were in process, Henry Ford entered politics for the first and only time in his life. Although Ford was a Republican, he had supported President Wilson for a second term in 1916 because of Wilson's efforts to keep the United States out of World War I.

"It is better to spend money for peace than preparedness," said Ford in explaining his position.

In the midterm election of 1918, the contest for

seats in Congress was very close. Although a presidential election occurs only every four years, one-third of the Senators and all of the Representatives are elected every two years, in the middle of the presidential term. The results of this midterm election often reflect the attitude of the people regarding the programs and activities of the President.

Although the war was still in progress, the end seemed near. President Wilson was already planning for the inclusion of a League of Nations in the peace treaty. He was anxious, therefore, to have the Democrats remain in control of Congress so that the peace treaty would be ratified with this clause included.

Although Michigan was a Republican state, the President was confident that Henry Ford could be elected on a Democratic ticket. Accordingly, he asked Ford to come to Washington to see him.

"You are the only man in Michigan who could be elected on the Democratic ticket," Wilson told Ford. "So I want you to run for the Senate. You can help bring about the peace we both so much desire."

Ford, though somewhat reluctant, agreed to run.

Running against Ford on the Republican ticket was Truman H. Newberry. He was a businessman and was backed by most of the conservative people in Michigan, who were against Wilson's liberal programs and social reforms.

Newberry made an active campaign and spent

The River Rouge Ford plant.

money freely. Henry Ford made no speeches at all and spent no money on the campaign. His popularity, however, among farmers and working people gave him a chance to win.

On election day Newberry won, though by a close margin. Ford in a recount of the vote had lost by only 2200 votes. There was an immediate outcry from the supporters of Ford that Newberry had violated the Corrupt Practices Act. This was the law limiting the amount of money that could be spent on an election.

On March 20, 1920, Newberry was found guilty of violating the Act. He was fined $10,000 and given a two-year prison term. Later on the sentence was reversed by the United States Supreme Court. Newberry then resigned from the Senate, and the Republican governor of Michigan appointed James B. Couzens, who was now prominent in politics, to succeed Newberry.

The result of the election of 1918 was a Republican victory in the Senate. The Democrats had forty-seven seats and the Republicans had forty-nine. If Ford had won the election, each party would have had an equal number of seats. But the Vice-president who presided over the Senate would have been a Democrat. In case of a tie, he would have the deciding vote. In addition, the heads of the committees would have been Democrats. In this event, President Wilson's fight to have the League of Nations included in the peace treaty might have been won.

Henry Ford might be considered vindictive because of his fight to have Newberry found guilty of violating the Corrupt Practices Act. Ford had little interest in politics other than his desire for peace. Perhaps the attacks on his son Edsel because he had not been in active service during the war angered the father, and in this way Ford retaliated.

Two years after the end of World War I, the United

States moved into an after-war depression. The sale of all automobiles declined in spite of lower prices. For a time, the Ford plant was closed. By 1921, Ford needed twenty-five million dollars to pay for the stock he had bought. With taxes and bonuses due, he needed fifty-eight million dollars. Banks throughout the country were eager to make Ford a loan, but he always had been against depending on banks for his financing.

"I don't think we have to go to the banks in order to get money," Ford told his associates. "The best thing is to start the plant going again. People will want to buy cars. That's where we'll get our money."

The depression, he was confident, was ending, and again there would be a market for cars.

By February, 1921, the Ford Company began shipping new cars to its dealers and marking them "collect." This was a regular procedure for all automotive companies. The only difference was that it was still a difficult time to sell cars. Most of the dealers, in spite of the fact that times were getting better, had cars left from previous orders, and the demand for automobiles was slow in starting.

However, Ford achieved his objectives. The dealers would lose their franchises if they did not accept the new cars. A few of them did refuse and either went out of business or switched to another company. The rest went to their local banks and borrowed money, and so Ford was able to pay his debts and have extra money. As it turned out, he did borrow money from the banks, though not directly.

In 1921, William S. Knudsen left the Ford Motor Company. This was a greater loss to Henry Ford than he realized at the time. In addition, other executives either were discharged or left the company at this time. For a while, Knudsen managed a company making automobile parts. Then Alfred P. Sloan, Sr., of General Motors offered Knudsen a job.

"How much should we pay you?" asked Sloan.

"Anything you like," answered Knudsen. "I'm here to seek an opportunity."

He started with an annual salary of thirty thousand dollars a year, although he had received fifty thousand from Ford.

Knudsen soon became head of the Chevrolet Division of General Motors. The Chevrolet Company had been started in 1911 by William C. Durant but became part of General Motors. Buick, Oldsmobile, and Pontiac were also part of General Motors now. But each was operated as a separate unit.

Knudsen used his experience at Ford to advance the sales of the Chevrolet. In 1921, when Knudsen had left the Ford Company, it was selling fifty-six percent of the automobiles sold in the United States. By 1925, the sales of the Ford cars began to decline, while Chevrolet sales advanced. Comfort and appearance in a car were demanded now and these were offered in a Chevrolet. In addition, the price of a Chevrolet was not much higher than a Ford car. In spite of the fact that Ford lowered the price of his car almost below cost, the Chevrolet continued to advance in sales.

The Sociological Department of the Ford Motor Company had also come to an end in 1921 with the resignation of Reverend Samuel Marquis. The relations of the clergyman with Sorenson had become increasingly strained, and Henry Ford usually took Sorenson's part. Sorenson was a necessity for Ford. Reverend Marquis and his department were luxuries. "The years from 1915 to 1921 were the happiest years in the history of Ford's," said Reverend Marquis sadly as his services ended.

Because of price increases and scarcity of material during the war, Ford was now determined to get control of the source of the materials he needed to manufacture his cars. In 1920, he began to purchase iron mines in Michigan. Large timber tracts were bought beginning with July, 1920. By 1923, he had control of coal mines in Kentucky and West Virginia. He even bought a small railroad line in Michigan, which had been operating at a loss. Ford not only made the line pay, but when he sold it later, he got seven times the amount he had paid for it.

In addition to owning raw materials, Ford began to manufacture what he needed for his cars. In 1923, he began the construction of trucks and barges for

Henry Ford (left) and coal miners at Stone, Kentucky mine.

transportation. He also started a new method of making plate glass, which in time was adopted by the other automotive companies. With Harvey S. Firestone, he fought against the British monopoly of the rubber industry. They both worked to develop the South American plantations that supplied crude rubber. This, however, was not successful. Artificial rubber was being manufactured by 1915. Eventually, Ford sold his plantations to Brazil. He had control now of a vast industrial empire, which stretched from Michigan to Brazil, and plants and buildings in thirty-three countries.

11

A time of humiliation

ALTHOUGH HENRY FORD GAINED full control of his company in 1919, in that same year he endured public humiliation. On June 22, 1919, in an editorial in *The Chicago Tribune*, Ford was called an "ignorant idealist" and an "anarchist." Ford immediately filed a suit for libel against the *Tribune* for a million dollars.

The trial began on May 12, 1919, in Mount Clemens, a little town about twenty-two miles from Detroit. Neither Chicago nor Detroit was considered the place for the trial. The little courthouse in Mount Clemens had to be remodeled to make room for the reporters and the curious public, as well as the huge staff for each side of the case.

If Ford had just sued on the term "anarchist," he would have won his case with no difficulty. But his libel suit included the whole editorial, and the case revolved about the attempt to prove that Ford was an "ignorant idealist."

The chief witness was Henry Ford himself. His cross examination began on July 14, 1919. The attorneys for the *Tribune* had no trouble in proving that Ford was "ignorant" in the field of general knowledge. He had little formal education, and his reading had been confined to technical material relating to the automotive industry.

Throughout the examination, Ford never lost his temper, though he was frequently goaded by the attorneys for the *Tribune*. He sat slumped forward in his chair, his chin cupped in his hand, his body moving from side to side, with one leg crossed over the other. He answered all questions patiently, and was never guarded in his replies. He admitted frankly that he was "ignorant about most things."

His ignorance seemed especially apparent in the field of American history. The questions that were asked Ford regarding the history of his country could have been answered by most grade school children. In an interview he had given to a reporter from the *Tribune* three years before, he had said, "History is more or less bunk. It's mostly tradition." This statement was repeated at the trial.

"I did not say it was bunk," he replied in answer to the statement. "It was bunk to me. I did not need it very bad."

The case went to the jury on August 14. The members of the jury were farmers. By nightfall, they had found the *Tribune* guilty of libel, and fined it six cents for damages.

The lawyers of both sides claimed victory. However, they both had lost the esteem and respect of the public. The *Tribune* was thought to have spoken spitefully. Ford was seen as a man painfully deficient in knowledge of everything except his own business. His image, however, was not changed for most of the people in the lower classes of society, for they, too, were neither educated nor informed. They still considered Ford to be the benefactor of the working class, and he received hundreds of letters of praise and encouragement after the trial.

Henry Ford listens to testimony at *Chicago Tribune* libel trial.

In 1950, when the papers of Henry Ford were being examined after the death of Mrs. Ford, one of the first letters discovered was one written to Henry Ford on July 30, 1941, by Colonel Robert R. McCormick, publisher of *The Chicago Tribune.*

"It occurs to me on this, our birthday," the letter began, "to write you and say I regret the editorial we published about you so many years ago. I only wonder why the idea never occurred to me before. . . . I am not planning to publish this myself, but you are perfectly welcome to use it in any way you wish."

It is to the great credit of Henry Ford that this vindication was never known to the public until the day it was discovered by those who were examining his papers. Evidently, he had not shown it to anyone except the members of his family or his close friends.

Ford's business continued to expand. In 1922, he acquired the Lincoln Motor Company of Detroit. It was headed by Henry M. Leland and his son Wilfred. Leland was a distinguished industrialist who had been interested in technical development ever since he had been a toolmaker in Springfield, Massachusetts. He had played an important part in the development of the Oldsmobile and also the Cadillac. In 1917, he had founded the Lincoln Company with his son Wilfred.

In October, 1921, the Lelands were almost bankrupt. To let the company fail would not only be disastrous for Henry Leland, who was now seventy-eight years old, but it would be bad for Detroit because of the unemployment that would result.

Ford was probably interested in producting a quality car as well as a cheap one, but he did nothing at first when the Lelands went into receivership. There are contrary accounts of how Ford in time got control of the Lincoln Company. For the most part, there were only verbal agreements between him and the Lelands.

According to the Ford account, the Lelands came to see Henry Ford at Fair Lane to discuss their problems. After they left, Mrs. Ford said to her husband, "Can't you do something to help them? It's a shame to see that company wrecked."

The Lelands, however, stated that Henry Ford asked them to come see him at his plant in Highland Park. This was followed by conferences at Fair Lane,

From left, Henry Leland, Mr. and Mrs. Wilfred Leland, Eleanor, Edsel, Clara, and Henry Ford.

which Mrs. Ford possibly overheard or was told.

There are different stories, too, about the agreements that were made after the conferences. Whatever the situation, the agreements were not written ones.

On February 4, 1922, at the receivership sale, Henry Ford made the only bid for the Leland plant. He offered eight million dollars for the property, and his offer was accepted. The members of both the Ford and Leland families were present, and they all seemed happy over the arrangement. The two companies would be united, but the Lelands were to continue to manage the Lincoln Company.

It was not long, however, before friction developed. Charles Sorenson, who was sent over from the Ford Company to check on methods of production, soon got into arguments with the Lelands. There were disputes, too, about full payment to stockholders and creditors, which the Lelands claimed Ford had promised to make. Ford insisted that his payment of eight million dollars was adequate.

The Lelands withdrew from the company on June 22, 1922. Ford paid the creditors of the Lincoln Company, but not the original stockholders. Altogether Ford paid about four million dollars in claims of creditors.

In this same year, Henry Ford was being well publicized in another field. In spite of the *Tribune* suit, he was still popular throughout the country. His folksiness made him a favorite in Michigan and other midwestern states. In the spring of 1922, a group of political leaders met in Dearborn and organized a "Ford for President" club. "We want Henry," was on their hatbands. Most of the members were business or professional men who had little knowledge of politics. Similar clubs were organized all over the country. A poll that was taken by *Collier's*, a popular magazine of the time, showed that Henry Ford had an eight-to-five lead over President Harding.

In the beginning of the movement, Ford said, "The idea is a joke." However, he did not stop the petitions to file his name in the Iowa primaries. Mrs. Ford was strongly opposed. She realized that her husband's entrance into a political campaign would only mean humiliation for him. "If Mr. Ford goes to Washington," she said, "I'll go to England."

Ford had no idea of what the Presidency required of a man. "Just correspondence and things like that," he said to his associates.

It would have been disastrous if he had been chosen as a candidate. By his own statements, Ford found reading difficult. Books "mussed up his mind." He could not make a speech. He knew little about political history. He was ill at ease in public, though friendly and easy with those he knew well.

After President Harding died on August 2, 1923,

the situation changed. Ford then went to Washington for an interview with Calvin Coolidge, who had succeeded Harding. After the interview, Ford issued a statement that said that he intended to support President Coolidge for President in 1924.

In the papers discovered after Mrs. Ford's death was the long telegram that President Coolidge sent to Ford after this announcement. The President expressed his "gratification" that Henry Ford "would not consider running against the present chief executive." He considered Mr. Ford a man of "far-reaching judgment regarding the public interest."

Some people thought that Ford might have been influenced in his decision by President Coolidge's statement that he was in favor of private ownership of Muscle Shoals.

During World War I, dams and plants had been built at Muscle Shoals, on the Tennessee River in northwestern Alabama to manufacture nitrates. After the war, a plan had been submitted to the Secretary of War to permit Muscle Shoals either to be leased or bought by a private company in order to continue the manufacture of nitrates. Henry Ford was one of those interested in securing Muscle Shoals. Not only did he want to use the nitrates to manufacture a much needed fertilizer, but after the war, the government was selling surplus property at salvage prices and Ford hoped to obtain Muscle Shoals at a bargain.

Senator George W. Norris of Nebraska led the fight to prevent private ownership of the project. The price Ford offered, said Norris, was less than what the plant would bring if sold as scrap. Norris wanted government operation of the project. Ford withdrew his offer in October, 1924, but it was fifteen years before Norris won his fight. As a result, the Tennessee Valley Authority (T.V.A.) was established, by which government dams controlled the flood waters of the Tennessee River and provided cheap electricity for the areas in the valley of the river.

Perhaps the *Tribune* suit aroused Ford's interest in making American history come alive. His first step in this direction was the restoration of the Wayside Inn in Sudbury, Massachusetts. The inn was built in 1686 and is the oldest existing inn in the United States. It had become famous through a book of poems, *Tales of a Wayside Inn*, written by Henry Wadsworth Longfellow.

Through the years, the Wayside Inn had decayed, until in 1923 Henry Ford bought the building and 2667 acres of ground and began the work of remodeling and refurnishing it in the style of the period in which it had flourished. Other buildings were bought or moved to the site. The most famous is the little red schoolhouse, well known because of the verses concerning "Mary's little lamb." There has been controversy as to whether either Mary or the lamb ever existed, but Ford did what he could to make the story an established fact.

This was the time, too, when Ford's association with Harvey S. Firestone, Thomas Edison, and John Burroughs was closest. Ford always enjoyed the out-of-doors. Beginning with 1918, he went on camping trips with his three friends. Trucks loaded with equipment to make the campers comfortable went along, though the three men did many of the camping chores. Sitting around the fireside in the evening and exchanging stories and experiences was their chief enjoyment.

The trips ended in 1924, partly because of the death of Burroughs in 1921, but also because of the publicity the trips received. "The trips were fun," said

Thomas Edison, back to camera. Facing camera (left to right) Harvey Firestone, Henry Ford, John Burroughs.

Ford, "but they attracted too much attention."

Ford's interest in history also extended to the area in which he lived. "I'm going to start a museum that will show just what actually happened years ago," he told one of his associates.

Ford began his collection for Greenfield Village about 1913, though in the beginning many of the items were stored. He had no theme in mind. Some of the things were collected for sentimental reasons. Others because he liked machinery and useful objects.

"I am collecting the history of our people with the things their hands made and used," he said. "A piece of machinery is like a book, if you can read it." Henry Ford himself had always been able to read "a piece of machinery" more easily than a book.

As time went on, Ford planned to have an "indoor-outdoor" museum, each contributing to the other. The outdoor museum, Greenfield Village, covers 260 acres and has more than one hundred buildings. It is a faithful reproduction of life in America from colonial times to the twentieth century. Most of the buildings are actual structures, brought to Dearborn and carefully rebuilt. A few are exact reproductions of the originals.

Along the streets of the Village are mills, shops, laboratories, historic buildings and homes, schools, a church, a town hall, and an inn. Many of the shops are in operation, and until 1969, classes were in session in the schools.

Until recently there was a real school system in Greenfield Village, whose students were a cross section of the people who live in Dearborn. The children attended classes from kindergarten through the sixth grade. After this they went to their local public or private school. But the children had their classes in the historic buildings. Each morning, they attended a nonsectarian service in the Martha-Mary chapel, in whose belfry is a bell made by Paul Revere's son.

Several of the buildings relate to Ford's own life. The house in which he was born; the shed from the house on Bagley Street, where he built and tried out his first car; the Scotch Settlement and the Miller Schools, which he attended as a boy; and Magill's jewelry shop, where he repaired watches, all were dismantled and rebuilt in the Village.

There are homes of famous people, from the log cabin birthplace of William Holmes McGuffey, famous for the readers that Henry Ford studied in school, to the more elaborate homes of Noah Webster and Wilbur and Orville Wright.

"I deeply admire the men who founded this country," said Ford, "and I think we ought to know more about them and how they lived and the force and courage they had."

The largest and most important group of buildings are those connected with the life of Thomas Alva Edison. Henry Ford had always held the inventor in high regard and wanted especially to honor him. In his laboratory in Menlo Park, New Jersey, Edison had produced the first incandescent lamp and other inventions and had worked out his system for electric lighting. Ford had the entire Menlo Park complex moved to Greenfield Village.

The Menlo Park Laboratory was dedicated on October 21, 1929, the fiftieth anniversary of the day Edison had first successfully tested his incandescent lamp. The building had been so faithfully reconstructed that several tons of New Jersey clay still surrounded it.

When Edison first entered the building, he said to Ford, "You've got it ninety-nine and nine tenths percent perfect."

"What's the matter with the other one tenth?"

"Oh," said Edison with a grin, "our floors were never this clean."

At the reenactment of the invention, Edison, who was eighty-two at the time, sat in the same yellow wooden chair from which he had watched the testing of his lamps. Henry Ford and President Hoover, who had come for the ceremony, stood in the background. No doubt, Henry Ford was more proud and pleased than the man who was being honored.

When Ford planned his indoor museum, he sent his architect to Philadelphia to purchase Independence Hall so that it could be reconstructed in Dearborn. The Philadelphia authorities firmly refused the request, so Ford ordered an exact reproduction. The center of the front of the Henry Ford Museum is an exact copy of Independence Hall. Duplicated on each side are Congress Hall and the old City Hall of Philadelphia. To the right of the entrance lobby is a chamber duplicating the room in which the Second Continental Congress met. On the other side is a duplication of the Supreme Court Chamber at the time Philadelphia was our national capital.

The Museum is divided into three sections. The

Thomas Edison (left) President Hoover (center) Henry Ford at the dedication of the reconstructed Menlo Park laboratory. Francis Jehl, longtime Edison employee (foreground).

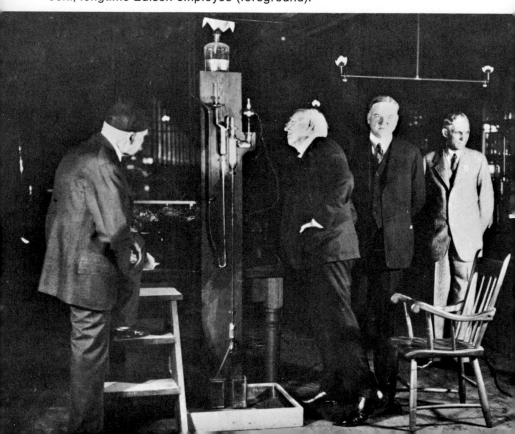

The Henry Ford Museum at Greenfield Village, soon after its completion.

Arts Gallery extends along the front, with exhibits of antique furniture, glassware, silver, porcelain, painting, watches, and clocks. More than fifty exquisite glass chandeliers reflect this beautiful display.

Back of this hall are five blocks of craft and trade shops, most of them in operation. The Mechanical Arts Hall covers an area of eight acres, and has exhibits relating to agriculture, industry, communication, illumination, and transportation. The vehicles connected with the development of the Ford car are of special interest. The second car Ford built; the Model T; the second Model A; the big and luxurious Model K; the huge racer, the *999;* and the "Selden buggy," are all there.

On the second floor of the Museum are three rooms dedicated to the memory of Henry Ford. Carefully protected are his first homemade tools; his first car; and a replica of his first engine. There are countless photographs, letters, records, gifts, and honors that he re-

147

ceived. Thus Henry Ford became the greatest collector of things that were American in this country. His museums are a constant denial of his statement that "history is more or less bunk."

It was at this time, also, that Ford actively promoted square dancing as a pleasant and healthful social activity. At a party with old friends in 1924, Henry Ford talked about the kind of dancing that was popular when he had courted his wife. The other guests tried to remember the "calls" and the steps of the dances.

"Do you realize, Henry Ford," said Clara, "that we have danced very little since we were married. It would do us both good to take it up again."

Ford liked the music and dance halls where the old-fashioned dances had been held. He and Clara were both good dancers, and they had gone to many dances in their youth. He thought the older dances were clean and healthful; dozens of people mingled. A girl danced with a number of partners in an evening instead of just one man. Parties of this type, he thought, would revive the old-time courtesies.

The first square dance sponsored by Henry Ford was a barn dance on Halloween. His interest continued and expanded from then for the next twenty years. At the Wayside Inn, he had engaged Mr. and Mrs. Benjamin Lovett of Boston to take charge of the social evenings at the Inn. Now he persuaded them to come to Dearborn to be in charge of evenings of dancing at the Engineering Laboratory at the River Rouge plant. A special floor was laid, and the dance hall was separated from the drafting rooms by a canvas curtain. Many a young engineer did his work to the tune of "Pop Goes the Weasel."

In time, the first dance hall was replaced by "Lovett Hall." It is in a large, two-story red brick building near the Ford Museum and is built in colonial style. The marble-floored lower hall and the upper rooms are handsomely decorated in crimson and ivory. A wide marble staircase leads to the ballroom, which has a teakwood floor. A four-piece orchestra was in constant attendance in Ford's time, for there were dancing classes for the adults as well. Lovett Hall is still beautiful and in demand today, and the local young people are proud to have their proms in this lovely setting.

The dances were always well attended. Employees had to be present and there were few in the social set at Grosse Pointe who would refuse to accept Henry Ford's invitation to an evening of square dancing in Lovett Hall.

There is an unpleasant side, however, to the story of Henry Ford at this period of his life, and that concerns his attacks on the Jews through his newspaper, *The Dearborn Independent.*

Even before the United States declared war in

1917, Ford had thought of establishing his own publication in order to express his views. At that time, he was backing the policies of President Wilson.

On January 11, 1919, the first issue of *The Dearborn Independent* appeared. It was a sixteen-page weekly, which sold for five cents a copy. The paper was not designed to promote the sale of Ford cars. He actually lost money on the publication, for it carried no paid advertising.

In May, 1920, *The Dearborn Independent* printed the first of a series of twenty articles against the Jews. They were described as a "menace" and accused of starting World War I "because they controlled the banks." The article further stated that the Jews, through secret organizations, were aiming to gain control of the commerce, finances, and governments of the world.

Resentment rose throughout the country, as the articles continued through ninety issues of *The Dearborn Independent.* Many of the Ford dealers complained because the publication of the articles was hurting their sales. The articles were discontinued for a time, but in 1924 *The Dearborn Independent* attacked the policies of Aaron Sapiro, a distinguished Chicago attorney, who was advocating farm cooperatives.

The result was a million dollar libel suit by Sapiro against *The Dearborn Independent* for defamation of character. In the trial, the editor, W. J. Cameron, was the chief witness. He blandly stated that he alone was responsible for the policies of his weekly, and that Henry Ford had never even read an advance copy of the paper.

The case was settled out of court. Ford published a personal apology to Aaron Sapiro and retracted all the statements made against the Jews. At the end of 1927, the publication of *The Dearborn Independent* came to an abrupt close. However, the fact that Ford permitted Cameron to take the blame rather than himself is as much a charge against him as the character of the articles that were written.

Although the whole affair has cast a blot on the memory of Henry Ford, the great majority of the American people at the time still had faith in him. His mistakes and his prejudices were those of the simple people themselves, and they were ready to forgive him.

12

The end of the Model T

By 1923, General Motors had become a close competitor of the Ford Motor Company. The Chevrolet was General Motors' best-selling car. Then when boom times started in 1925, the sale of the Chevrolet increased while the sale of the Model T declined.

But in spite of pressure from his executives and dealers, Henry Ford would not agree that the end of the Model T was drawing near. Because Edsel was younger and less narrow-minded, he differed in this from his father. Edsel was far more interested in the styling of a car. This became the chief point of argument between the two men.

But even Edsel could not convince Henry Ford that the Model T had outlived its time. The first real bitter jokes about the car were now being told. "Why is a Ford like a bathtub? Because you hate to be seen in one," was one of the jokes most repeated.

People still wanted low-priced cars, but now they wanted them with style and comfort as well. In the past, Ford had said, "You can have the Model T in any color as long as it is black," and his statement had been accepted with a laugh. Now car buyers wanted color in their cars. They also wanted comfort and convenience.

There had been some improvements in the Model T. There were electric headlights, a Klaxon horn and curved fenders. The biggest improvement came in 1919 when an electric self-starter was added. Cranking the Model T by hand had been a fearsome task.

The Model T still sold well, though the Chevrolet was closing the sales gap. Owners still said, "It takes you there, and it gets you back." Ford answered his critics by saying, "The only thing we need to worry about is the best way to make more cars."

By 1926, even though business was still booming, the production of the Model T dropped by a quarter of a million cars, and the sale of the Chevrolet was within a few thousand of the Ford car. Another threat to the sale of the Model T was that people were buying used cars in more expensive models. For a little less money than the cost of a new Model T, one could buy a used Buick, and for the difference have the worn parts replaced. In that case, a car owner would have a car far more attractive and modern than the Model T. It was true, the Model T apparently would last forever, but who in 1926, except a backwoods farmer, wanted anything that would last forever?

In the summer of 1926, some changes were made

in the appearance of the Model T, and it was even offered for sale in fancy colors, like "fawn gray," and "Highland green." Then prices were cut below cost, but still the sales declined. Dealers became afraid now, and some of them gave up their Ford franchises and switched to General Motors. In spite of this, Henry Ford still stubbornly resisted any suggestion that he stop making the Model T. Edsel, though strongly in favor of making the change, would not oppose his father. "He's the boss," said Edsel.

Then on May 25, 1927, Ford made another dramatic gesture by announcing that no more Model T's would be made, though parts would be manufactured for five years. The following day, Car Number 15,000,-000 rolled off the assembly line. The number 15,000,-

Henry and Edsel Ford pose in fifteen millionth Model T.

000 was painted in silver on its black side (though actually 7,033 more Model T's were made after this).

Nothing was said about the design of the new car, and probably no other product, then and since, was awaited with so much interest. Ford had money, a capable staff, and experience in designing as well as complete confidence in his ability to produce a car that would be honest and would capture the market. But he also had much against him. Unlike General Motors, he had no means for trying out his models. The public highways instead of testing grounds were used by Ford for trying out his cars. Nor did he have a centralized laboratory or research department, which were common with the other companies.

Ford was a mechanical genius and did much to design the engine of the new car. The design of the body was left to Edsel. "We have a pretty good man in my son," Ford said with pride he did little to conceal. "He knows how a car ought to look, and he has mechanical horse sense, too."

Ford tested the first car himself. He drove it roughshod over a field. What faults he found in the car were corrected.

The official announcement of the new car was made by Edsel on August 10, 1927. It would be called Model A.

A tremendous job of retooling faced the plant. All new parts had to be made. A whole new assembly line

155

had to be devised. On Thursday, October 20, 1927, the serial number of the first Model A was stamped by hand. The car, however, was not sold but was used for testing.

By early December, there were full page advertisements of the new car. Almost 400,000 had already been ordered, so much confidence did the public have in a Ford product. There would be seven different types of cars made, and they would be made in different colors. Safety glass in the windshields and hydraulic brakes would be features, and the price would be lower

Henry and Edsel Ford with Model A in one of the company's showrooms, 1927.

than the current Chevrolet. The plant was unable to keep up with the orders, and some of those who were able to get an order filled made a good profit on the resale of their cars.

"Henry's made a lady out of Lizzie," was said after the new Model A was produced. This was the final Ford joke.

13

Labor troubles

THE STOCK MARKET in the United States crashed on October 29, 1929. This is generally considered as the date when the Depression began, though there were many causes other than the sudden and terrific fall in the price of stocks.

The stock market crash had little immediate effect on those who were directly involved. President Hoover and his cabinet were confident that the situation was only temporary. "Prosperity is just around the corner," was their favorite slogan.

But prosperity did not return. As time went on, unemployment increased; purchasing power declined; factories closed; banks failed; people lost their homes because they were unable to pay their mortgages; the farmers lost their farms for the same reason; each condition made the other worse. The economic situation was just as bad in the other countries of the world.

Henry Ford refused to accept the realities of the Depression. He made public statements that shocked

158

many people because they seemed so callous. He said the Depression was "wholesome," and that the people would profit by the "illness."

It is difficult to understand Henry Ford's attitude toward the Depression, because he himself was from humble beginnings, and he had always been interested in the problems and welfare of the laboring man. Perhaps because of his great wealth and the isolated way in which he now lived, he was too far removed from the sufferings of the people. He may not have seen the breadlines; the idle, hopeless people in the streets; or even understood the "hunger march" on his own River Rouge plant.

In spite of his statements, Ford was public-spirited in the beginning. He tried price cutting and plant expansion in order to increase purchasing power. He also raised wages. Other automotive companies also lowered prices.

The Ford Motor Company had changed to its new Model A shortly before the stock market crash. The new car had sold well in the beginning mainly because it had been so long awaited. But by 1930, the automotive industry as a whole began to decline. Cars were a luxury that most people could do without. The incomes of the companies declined more than the national income, and the used-car market was glutted with unsold cars. Nearly one-third of the dealers went out of business. Many small automotive companies disappeared. Ford, General Motors, Chrysler, Packard, Nash, Studebaker, and Hudson were the only automobile companies that survived the Depression.

The worst year was 1932. Only one-fifth as many cars were produced then as in 1929. Ford now had to reduce his force and cut wages. The other companies did the same. By 1934, Ford began to make a modest profit. Until 1927 his Company had made nine hundred million dollars in profit. During the three worst years of the Depression, he lost one hundred and twenty-five million. So he was far from bankruptcy.

In 1932, Franklin Delano Roosevelt, the Democratic candidate, defeated Herbert Hoover for the Presidency. Before 1932, when he was governor of New York, Roosevelt had stated that if people were deprived of a means of livelihood through no fault of their own, the government owed them a livelihood. He had started many programs in New York to bring this about and thus fight the Depression.

When Roosevelt was nominated by the Democratic party for the Presidency, he had promised a "New Deal" for the American people. By this he meant that the small businessman, farmer, and the workingman would get a better hand of cards with which to play.

The result of the election was an overwhelming victory for Roosevelt, and with him many other Democrats were elected. During the period called the "Hundred Days," from the time of the inauguration of

160

Roosevelt until Congress adjourned on June 16, many bills were rapidly passed to relieve the economic and social distress in the country. Slowly conditions began to improve. It was from 1932 on that the Ford Company began to make a profit on its cars.

In the second half of Roosevelt's first term, important laws were passed regarding labor. The National Labor Relations Act (N.L.R.A.) gave unions the right of "collective bargaining." This meant that representatives of management had to meet with representatives of unions to discuss grievances. The

Clara and Henry Ford in their Fair Lane home.

Act prevented many strikes. The National Labor Relations Board (N.L.R.B.) saw that the terms of the Act were carried out.

On the day the N.L.R.A. was signed, Henry Ford said, "We know that President Roosevelt wants to do the right and helpful thing, but I doubt if the government knows how to run a business." The heads of other automotive industries had the same opinion.

Another act, the National Industrial Recovery Act (N.I.R.A.) also had been passed. By this, various industries agreed to a code which set minimum prices for their products as well as minimum wages for their employees. The purpose of this Act was to prevent industries from lowering prices and making up their losses by lowering wages.

Ford refused to sign the N.I.R.A. agreement for the automotive industry. (He knew his books would be examined. All of the stock was held by his family. He did not want an invasion of his privacy.) He felt he was doing more for his employees than the code required. "I have never bargained with my men. I have always bargained for them," he stated.

Henry Ford's attitude toward labor at this time was largely influenced, it is thought, by one of his executives, Harry Bennett, who had come to the Ford Plant in 1918. He worked first in the commercial art department, but advanced rapidly. However, he was not an important factor at Ford's until after 1927.

Bennett was an athlete. He had been a former fighter in the ring and an ex-sailor. He was still a good boxer and was always physically fearless. He was a short, stocky man with sharp features, hard blue eyes, and scars from fighting on his cheeks and nose. His dark brown hair was carefully combed to hide his increasing baldness. He always dressed neatly though rather gaudily.

There were legends about Bennett as he grew more important at Ford's. He had three homes, including a fine one on Grosse Isle. All were supposed to have secret exits. Bennett was definitely connected with the underworld, and this was the time when Detroit, because of prohibition, was a center for gangsters. Much liquor was being smuggled in from Canada.

Bennett always carried a revolver. In his small, rather plain office at the Rouge plant he practiced marksmanship. He would tilt back in his chair with one leg on his desk, and fire rapidly at a line of pencils or other targets. He was a fine marksman, and once had shot a cigar from between the teeth of a visitor.

Bennett always claimed that he got "peanuts" for a salary. But he had many ways of adding to his income. His three homes were not only built but were maintained by Ford, and there were numerous funds which he controlled without accounting.

Henry Ford liked Bennett personally because as Ford said, "Harry gets things done." There was no investigation as to how Bennett "got things done." Ford might have been attracted to Bennett because he had a type of toughness that Ford would have liked to see in his own decent and highly civilized son Edsel.

Bennett earned his hire at Ford's. His title was Director of Personnel, but he was more like a chief of police. He was industrious and attentive to details. He kept no records and was responsible only to Henry Ford. They saw each other every morning, and in addition they frequently drove around the plant. Usually Ford telephoned Bennett in the evening before retiring. Ford called Bennett his "loyal right arm," and Bennett said with some truth, "I was closer to him than his son."

It is hard to understand the change in attitude of Henry Ford toward his son. In Edsel's childhood, his father had been completely devoted to him, and proud of his son's ability as he grew up.

The devotion probably continued in later years, but there was no real understanding of Edsel by his father. Edsel was upright, had high ideals, and was public-spirited. He was just and considerate in his dealings with other people, and they regarded him with warm affection. Henry Ford also was honest and idealistic, but he thought his son was weak because he was not tough enough with those he dealt with in business. "He wanted to make Edsel in his own image," said Sorenson.

One of Bennett's chief duties was to protect Ford's grandchildren. There were constant threats of kidnapping. Bennett not only knew of these, but through his connections with the underworld, he could prevent the deed. Ford told him, "Never mind the plant. We can rebuild that. But we've got to make sure nothing happens to the children." Detroit was a jungle at this time, and Bennett never concealed his relations with the hoodlums who dominated the city.

Bennett was hated and dreaded by most of those in the Ford plant. He was Ford's hatchet man, and he seemed to take pleasure at times in firing those who were thought to be undesirable or who had crossed

Henry Ford confers with Harry Bennett.

his own path. Bennett was disliked by Sorenson, although he often worked with him. Edsel and the chief executives at the plant detested Bennett. He was also disliked by Mrs. Ford. Once she said to Sorenson, "This man Bennett has so much control over my husband, and he is ruining my son's health."

Labor troubles began for the Ford Motor Company after the election of President Roosevelt. Harry Bennett was largely responsible for Ford's attitude regarding the new movements in labor and his consequent encounters with organized labor.

Although there had been much new legislation benefitting the workingman in the beginning of the Roosevelt administration, there had been no change in the organization of labor. The American Federation of Labor (A.F.L.) was the only national organization of laborers. However, the A.F.L. was made up almost exclusively of various craft unions of skilled workers such as the carpenters, masons, and electricians.

Up to this time, the A.F.L. had ignored the demands of unskilled and semi-skilled labor in getting improvements for workingmen other than the skilled workers in the craft unions. The dissatisfaction was especially prevalent in the automotive industry, where mass production was the rule and the majority of the workers were unskilled.

Finally, under the leadership of John L. Lewis, in 1935, a new labor organization, the Congress for

Industrial Organization (C.I.O.), was formed. It was made up of various unions of unskilled workers. The members of the automotive industry were organized into the United Auto Workers, or the U.A.W.

During the Depression, the radical elements in the labor field pushed forward and tried to make the labor unions communistic. The Ford factory at Rouge was the target for the Communists because it was the largest plant and the symbol to them of capitalism.

The Communist elements within the labor movement in Detroit were eager to have a clash with the police so that they could win public sympathy. On Monday, March 7, 1932, they arranged a "hunger march" to the gates of Ford's Rouge plant. They purposely refrained from getting a permit for their march in order to come into conflict with the police. On the way to their meeting place, they jammed the streetcars and refused to pay their fares, shouting, "Charge it to Ford."

The men formed in a mile-long line and marched to the Dearborn employment office. The police tried to make them disperse and then used tear gas. However, the March winds blew the gas back in the faces of the police. There was a free-for-all fight after this in which the outnumbered police got the worse of the encounter.

Finally the fire department came to the aid of the police and turned fire hoses on the demonstrators. More police arrived. Shots were fired and there was a bloody battle. When it ended, four of the marchers had been killed and about twenty wounded. Policemen and firemen were also injured, but none were killed, for only the police had used firearms.

As soon as the fight started, Bennett had rushed out to speak to the marchers. He was greeted with a shower of bricks and knocked unconscious. If he had not fallen, he might have been killed.

On Saturday, there was a big funeral for the men who had been killed. The matter was brought before the N.L.R.B., but it was newly organized at the time. Neither Ford nor the police were held responsible by the N.L.R.B.

By the spring of 1937, the U.A.W., under the provisions of the N.L.R.A., had called strikes and secured contracts from General Motors and Chrysler. "Ford next," was the slogan of the U.A.W.

In May, 1937, the city of Dearborn gave union men the right to stand outside the gates of the Rouge plant and distribute leaflets. But the Rouge was like a fortress. It had its own strong-armed guard, commanded by Bennett, to protect the plant. Ford had said, "We will never recognize the U.A.W. nor any other union."

On May 26, U.A.W. organizers went to the Rouge plant at shift-changing time. A bridge led over Miller Road to Gate Number 4. This had been built to prevent traffic tie-ups at shift-changing time, but the bridge was also used by the public.

Two officials of the U.A.W., Walter Reuther and Richard Frankensteen, went on the bridge to oversee proceedings. With them was a minister, Reverend Raymond P. Sandford. At one end of the bridge were a number of big, powerfully built men. "This is Ford property! Get out of here!" they shouted.

The union men turned to withdraw, but at the other end of the overpass they were blocked by approaching guards, all of whom were armed. Caught between the two groups, the union men were knocked down and beaten. Reuther's body and face were severely kicked. Others at the gates also were attacked,

Walter Reuther (left) and Richard Frankensteen after the "battle of the bridge," May 26, 1937.

and many were seriously injured.

Most newspapers were opposed to the C.I.O., and probably a story favorable to Ford would have been written. However, the guards made the mistake of also attacking the reporters and tearing up films. Enough vivid pictures were saved, however, of the "battle of the overpass," to serve as convincing testimony when the matter was brought before the N.L. R.B. Ford was ordered to "cease and desist" from discouraging union membership in his plants. Men who had been fired were given their jobs again. When Ford was questioned, he denied any knowledge of what had taken place.

In a letter, Harry Bennett stated, "If the N.L.R.B. orders an election, we will hold one. . . . The C.I.O. will win, of course. . . . But they won't get anything."

Bennett was wrong.

On April 1, 1941, 50,000 workers on their own accord went on strike at the Rouge plant. They left the plant in a body and marched through the streets of Detroit, carrying banners and chanting their slogans.

In order to prevent strikebreakers from working at the plant, the U.A.W. stationed cars filled with men at each end of the five roads leading to the plant. "The only way one could get into the Rouge was by parachute from a plane," said one writer.

Bennett telegraphed at once to President Roosevelt, "Communist leaders are actively directing this lawlessness." But the President did not answer the telegram.

Few strikebreakers got into the plant, and those who remained began to run wild and destroy property. Henry Ford at first wanted to arm the guards and use tear gas, but Edsel prevented this. On the third day of the strike, at Edsel's insistence, Ford agreed to negotiate.

The strike ended on April 11, and work was resumed two days later. Elections for the bargaining agent were held on May 21. The C.I.O. got seventy percent of the votes. Contract negotiations began soon after, and a contract was signed on June 20, 1941.

"We have decided to go the whole way," said Ford. He agreed to terms that were more generous than

Ford employees ballot for bargaining agent, May 21, 1941.

those of any of his competitors. The C.I.O. was to be the sole bargaining agent. Discharged workers were to return to their jobs and receive back wages. Union fees were to be deducted by the company from the men's wages. A union shop would be permitted.

Many wondered why Ford had done this. Was it just because he wanted to do the dramatic thing and get favorable publicity? Since the N.L.R.B. elections, he had begun listening to the reasoning of his wife and son. Mrs. Ford had told him that she would leave him if he did not sign the contract. Also, the United States, Ford felt, was going to be involved soon in World War II. He knew that if his plant were paralyzed in the midst of a war, he would be condemned. In spite of Ford's opinion regarding war, he was a patriot and would work to defend his country. Perhaps, most of all, he could not bear to see his beloved plant idle when there was so much to do.

14

The end of an era

PEARL HARBOR, OUR GREAT naval base in the Hawaiian Islands, was attacked by Japanese airplanes on Sunday, December 7, 1941. The following day, the United States declared war on Japan. Because of the alliance between Germany, Italy, and Japan, Germany and Italy declared war on the United States on December 12, and the following day, we declared war on these two powers.

Before the war in Europe started in 1939, Henry Ford was in sympathy with the isolationists in this country, such as Charles Lindbergh and Colonel Robert McCormick, the publisher of *The Chicago Tribune*. Ford, who had received a decoration from Adolph Hitler in 1934, refused to accept any contracts from European countries for war material.

But war in Europe, as in World War I, and defense of the United States were two different things for Henry Ford. As the conflict progressed, Henry Ford, more than any other industrialist, made it possible for the United States to meet the large scale production demanded by the global war.

Ford began to think about producing airplanes in October, 1940. However, building an automobile on an assembly line was very different from building a bomber. The B-24 bomber had 488,193 separate parts. Furthermore, it was impossible to "freeze" the construction of a bomber as the design was constantly being changed.

Sorenson and Edsel, with some of the Ford engineers, went to San Diego to see how Consolidated Aircraft was building bombers. The company was turning out a bomber a day, but the Air Force wanted many thousands built each year.

General Hap Arnold of the Army Air Corps autographs a B-24 *Liberator* bomber as Henry Ford (right) watches.

To Sorenson, the men at Consolidated Aircraft seemed to be falling all over each other. After carefully checking their procedures, he went to his hotel room and worked all night laying out a plan for building a bomber on an assembly line. The building to house it would have to be a mile long and a quarter of a mile wide in order to make this possible.

The River Rouge plant would not be adequate for such a project, so Ford decided to build a new plant to be called Willow Run. Work on the new factory began almost immediately. It was near Ypsilanti, a little college town about twenty miles west of Dearborn. The proportions seemed so fantastic and the work of construction so slow that the scoffers began to call it, "Will-It Run."

Production of the Liberator bombers began at Willow Run in May, 1942. The area around the plant was a hodgepodge of buildings. Ford was unwilling to provide proper housing for the thirty thousand workers. He said it would concentrate people where they might be bombed. In addition, he thought that the war would soon be over. For the most part, the workers lived in tents, trailers, and other makeshift housing.

In spite of the huge plant, the bomber production at Willow Run, in the beginning, was far less than expected. Many changes were made by the War Department, and there was a constant turnover in the work force because of the drafting of the men employed. It was not until the end of 1943, that adequate production was achieved.

Until 1938, when Ford was seventy-five years old, his health had been excellent. He could climb stairs, easily, jump over a fence into the seat of his car, and was mentally alert. He had his first slight stroke in 1938, but there was not much change in his health. However, in 1941, he had a second stroke, which had more serious effects. He was slower in his gait after that. He became cold easily. He suffered from lapses of memory, and he was often cross and suspicious.

The strained relations between Edsel Ford and his father after Herry Bennett became influential affected Edsel's health. He developed stomach ulcers. He had the same philosophy as his father regarding the type of car to be built, and the early relations with labor. The difference between father and son was in the character of the two men, and this difference affected the way they administered the business. Henry Ford believed in the leadership of one man. "That's the only way to get things done—one man rule," he said. Edsel sought the opinion of others.

Henry Ford grew more autocratic as he increased his ownership of the stock in his company. Edsel was orderly and democratic. Henry had greater talent than Edsel, but the industry, as it grew more complex, needed a man of Edsel's type rather than his father's. The men at Ford's thought Edsel was a "gentleman."

Henry Ford II, Edsel, and Henry Ford.

Many of them stayed with Ford because they expected Edsel to run the plant one day.

After 1918, Edsel had the title of President of the Ford Motor Company, but he never had the full power. His father would emphasize his son's position by saying to executives, "Do whatever he says." Then he would often countermand Edsel's orders.

At times Edsel took issue with his father, but usually he did what his father wished. "After all, my father built this business," he said. As a result, the executives did not have full confidence in Edsel, for they knew he did not have the final word. Henry Ford was proud of his son, but he wished to make him over in his own image. As Harry Bennett grew more and more powerful, this desire of Henry Ford to change

177

the character and personality of his son grew stronger.

In the spring of 1943, Edsel's stomach ulcers became cancerous. In May, he became ill from undulant fever contracted by drinking unpasturized milk from his father's farm. Henry Ford refused to believe that his son was gravely ill.

Edsel died at home on May 26, 1943. All of Detroit was deeply sorrowful, for the people respected him, and he had played a prominent part in the life of the community. At the funeral, Henry Ford seemed composed, though he might have been hiding his deep grief. Bennett did not go to the funeral, for he knew how Edsel despised him. Sorenson broke down, though he also had tormented Edsel. But Sorenson knew by this time that his own days with Ford were numbered.

After Edsel's death, Henry Ford wanted to take over the presidency, in spite of his poor health and his age. He was eighty years old in 1943. He was elected president on June 1, 1943, though it was considered only a temporary position. Bennett began to fire those who had taken Edsel's part or were close to him, and Ford did nothing to stop this. Perhaps he was too old, or numbed with grief and his mistaken disappointment in his son.

There was increasing hostility between Sorenson and Bennett by this time. Finally, in November, Sorenson told Ford that he wished to retire at the beginning of 1944 and go to Florida.

"I guess there's something else besides work," said Ford, with no apparent protest. This was strange, considering that Sorenson had worked for Ford for forty years and had contributed substantially to the success of the mass-production methods of the plant.

Sorenson did not resign in January, though the tension between him and Bennett continued. Finally, Ford, no doubt influenced by Bennett, asked Sorenson to resign in March. He stated that Sorenson was trying to become president of the company.

"The wizard of Dearborn has slashed off his right arm," said the *Detroit Free Press.*

To reporters in Miami, Sorenson said, "I am compelled to take a much needed rest." However, three months later, Sorenson apparently was well enough to accept the presidency of the Willys-Overland Motor Company and continue there with war work.

In spite of Bennett's influence with Henry Ford, his grandson, Henry II, who was twenty-six at this time, was in the best position to succeed his grandfather as the President of the Ford Motor Company. His very name gave him the first right, and he was backed strongly by his mother and grandmother. Both these women were taking positive stands now in regard to the company, and the large number of shares of voting stock that they owned gave them power.

A few months after the death of his father, Henry II was released from service in the United States Navy.

He had always had a keen interest in the automotive industry and had kept up with the developments at the Ford plants. He now moved into his father's office at the Rouge and kept some of his staff. As much as possible, he avoided both Sorenson and Bennett.

By the late summer of 1945, after Sorenson had resigned, both Clara and Eleanor Ford insisted that young Henry be made president of the company. "If you don't agree," Mrs. Edsel Ford told her father-in-law, "I shall sell my stock."

Finally Henry Ford agreed to resign, and on September 21, 1945, as Harry Bennett, livid with anger, watched, Henry II was made president by the board of directors. The first Henry Ford, now an old and bewildered man, was almost led from the office.

Young Henry Ford's career had been colorless up to this time. He had never been a good student and had left Yale University before his graduation. He was a mild and modest young man, though he appeared to have more force than his father. He was athletic in build and almost six feet tall. By this time he was married to Anne McDonnell, who came from a wealthy and socially prominent New York family. The McDonnells were Roman Catholics, and Henry had become a Roman Catholic before his marriage to Anne.

As soon as he took over the company, Henry II fired one thousand employees of Ford's. Some were not capable of holding their jobs, but most of them had been either enemies of Edsel Ford or were appointees of Harry Bennett. The first one to go was Harry Bennett himself.

The question of inheritance taxes began to concern the Ford family long before the death of Edsel Ford. The inheritance tax, which was passed in 1916, was moderate in the beginning. Through the years, however, the rates increased, especially for large fortunes. By August 30, 1945, the tax was seventy percent of all inheritances over $50,000,000.

The sudden death of Henry Ford and his heirs would mean that large blocks of stock would have to be sold in order to pay the tax. In this way, the Ford family would lose control of the company. To offset this, the Ford Foundation was established on January 15, 1936. In time, it received the bulk of the Ford wealth, but still left the control of the company in the hands of the family.

To create the Foundation, the Ford stock was divided into ninety-five percent of Class A stock and five percent of Class B stock. The Class A stock, which carried no voting powers, was turned over to the Foundation; but all inheritance taxes had to be paid from the sale of this stock. The Class B stock with its voting power, was held by the family.

Henry Ford was reluctant in the beginning to establish the Foundation. Not only did he distrust lawyers and legal methods of evasion, but he was opposed to the organized giving of charity. "I have no patience with professional charities," he said. He was a generous man, and there are hundreds of instances of giving on his part, but he preferred to deal with individuals rather than groups. He wished to help others to help themselves. "Charity is no substitute for reform," was his opinion. In the end, the tax situation made him agree to the Foundation, though "charity" is only a small part of the manner in which the foundation funds are used.

By early in 1947, Henry Ford, no longer under the influence of Bennett, had become pleased with the progress of his grandson as president of the Ford Company. In April, the Fords returned to Dearborn from their winter home in Georgia. On Monday, April 7, they visited the Rouge plant and examined the model of the new car. Ford was feeling fine and was pleased with the model.

There had been prolonged and heavy rains in Dearborn, and the River Rouge had been rising steadily. By the evening of April 7, it was thirty feet above its normal level. Although the flood waters did not reach the main house, the power plant on the banks of the river was flooded. As a result, there was neither heat nor electricity at Fair Lane, and the telephone wires were down.

The Fords retired early. There were only wood fires to keep the big rooms warm, and flickering candles or oil lamps for light. About 11:15 P.M. Ford called for his wife. He was quite ill, he said, and his throat felt dry. Quickly Mrs. Ford sent a chauffeur to bring a doctor from the Ford Hospital. At 11:40 P.M., Henry Ford died, just a few minutes before the doctor arrived. His death was due to a cerebral hemorrhage.

Messages of sympathy came to the family from great industrial and political leaders all over the world, among them President Truman. On April 9, more than one hundred thousand people filed past the coffin in the Recreation Hall of Greenfield Village. Although it was raining heavily, thousands of mourners filled St. Paul's Cathedral in Detroit and the streets around it for the funeral. Only statements repeating Henry Ford's achievements were printed in the newspapers. The world forgot the mistakes in judgment he had made, and the accounts told only of his great contributions to the industrial development of the world.

"He had the dream"

AFTER THE DEATH OF Clara Ford in September, 1950, Fair Lane was examined for papers or anything else relating to the life of Henry Ford. His wife had lived very quietly after the death of her husband in only a few rooms of the big house.

To their great astonishment, the examiners found that fifty-two of the fifty-six rooms in Fair Lane were crammed with papers, photographs, and other material relating to the life of the Fords. Almost everything connected with his business or personal life had been kept by Henry Ford.

This vast supply of material was a tremendous find for the examiners, for not only did they learn the details of the life of the Fords, but they had a vivid picture of life in the United States for nearly three-quarters of a century. The material has now been classified and filed and is the basis for the Ford Archives, now housed in the Ford Museum.

In 1956, the Ford Motor Company gave the University of Michigan Henry Ford's home, Fair Lane, and about 210 acres of ground. With the gift of the real estate, the University also received a grant of $6,500,-000. There were no restrictions placed on the use of the house and grounds or the money that was given. Fair Lane is now used as a Conference Center by the University. Contributions of money and furnishings are being received to restore the home and grounds to their original beauty.

Henry Ford was a man of great contrasts in character and personality. "He was like a common man," it is said, "but a most uncommon man." He was a man who was modest and shy in public, yet he gave interviews readily, talked at great length to reporters, and liked being in the headlines.

He was friendly and on a first-name basis with his employees, at least in the beginning of his industry, and yet became the harshest driver of men in the automotive industry. He was kind and personally charitable in hundreds of unknown incidents, but on the other hand, he was strangely callous to the sufferings of people during the Depression.

Ford was contradictory in many of his statements and acts, yet he hewed to the line regarding his idea of the best type of car to be made and brooked no opposition. He was devoted to his son when he was young and proud of what he did, but almost cruel in his attitude toward Edsel in his later years.

Henry Ford's faults of character, however, belonged more to his later years, and these might have been brought on by the public humiliation he suffered in the *Tribune* suit and the ridicule of his Peace Ship, as well as through the influence of Harry Bennett. What Henry Ford contributed to the American way of life will last longer than the memory of his personality and character.

"He had the dream," Henry Ford's associates said of him. His dream was to produce an automobile that was sturdy in build, easy to repair, low in cost, and reliable in performance. It was to be a car within the means of the workingman and the small farmer.

Through Ford's mechanical genius and persistence, an automobile, the Model T, was produced which met these specifications. He started mass production of this car and it affected industries throughout the world, and changed the whole economy and way of life in this country. He doubled the wage scale for his employees and thus raised the standard of living in the United States and eventually in most of the countries of the world.

But Henry Ford's "dream" encompassed more than the design and construction of an automobile for the masses. Although it is said he showed "a streak of meanness" in his later life, in reality, he was an idealist. He wanted his employees to become Americans, to live properly, and to have themselves and their children educated. Although his Sociological Department had some faults, it did help to make living conditions better for the Ford workers and their families. Ford's Highland Park plant was a model of cleanliness, beauty, and safety. He spent a fortune in making history come alive in Greenfield Village and the Ford Museum.

Henry Ford's efforts to bring about world peace through his Peace Ship brought ridicule, but today there has been public apology for that ridicule. Henry Ford was an advocate of the simple life in his home, with his square dances, his love of birds and the out-of-doors, and his dislike of the display of wealth and snobbery. With the rank and file of the American people, everything that "Henry" did was either "smart" or "good," and his achievements will be remembered when his faults are long forgotten.

Great wealth in itself meant little to Henry Ford. Once Upton Sinclair asked him, "Does the possession of wealth make you any happier?"

"Of course," said Ford. "I can do things with it exactly as I want that I could not do otherwise."

BIBLIOGRAPHY

Burlingame, Roger, *Henry Ford*. New York, Alfred A. Knopf, Inc., 1955.

Ford Motor Company, *Ford at Fifty: 1903-1953*. New York, Simon & Schuster, Inc., 1953.

Garrett, Garet, *The Wild Wheel*. New York, Pantheon Books, 1952.

Nevins, Allen and Hill, Frank Ernest, *Ford: The Times, the Man, and the Company*. New York, Charles Scribner's Sons, 1954.

——— *Ford: Expansion and Challenge: 1915-1933*. New York, Charles Scribner's Sons, 1957.

——— *Ford: Decline and Rebirth: 1933-1962*. New York, Charles Scribner's Sons, 1963.

Olson, Sidney, *Young Henry Ford*. Detroit, Wayne State University Press, 1963.

Sward, Keith, *Legend of Henry Ford*. New York, Russell & Russell Publishers, 1948.

White, Lee Strout, *Farewell to Model T*. New York, G. P. Putnam's Sons, 1963.

188

Addams, Jane 110

Bennett, Harry 162-66, 177-80, 181, 186
Benz car 38, 40
Brayton gas engine 38, 83
Bryan, William Jennings 110
Burroughs, John 91-92, 110, 142-43

car production in U.S. (1901) 56
car racing 39-40, 58-59, 61-62, 71-72
Chevrolet car 130-31, 152
Cooper, Tom 60-61, 63
Couzens, James 64-66, 68-69, 74, 76, 115-16, 124-25

depressions in U.S. (1914) 99-100, 104; (after World War I) 128-29; (1929) 159-60
Detroit (1879) 19-20; (early 1900's) 54; (1913) 93-94
Detroit Automobile Company 50-53
Detroit Drydock Company 22
Dodge brothers 64-65, 123-24
Duryea car 33, 39, 40, 49

Edison, Thomas Alva 46-48, 110, 142, 144-45
Edison Company 30, 46, 50

Fair Lane, Ford's final home 120-22, 184-85
Firestone, Harvey 91-92, 132, 142
Flower Brothers machine shop, Ford's second job in Detroit 20-21

Ford, Clara Bryant (Mrs. Henry Ford):
courtship and marriage 25-30
death 184
diary and letters 53-55
opposes "Ford for President" movement 139
opposes Peace Ship 110
supports Henry's experiments 34-35
Ford, Edsel (Henry's son):
attacked for not serving in World War I 118
birth 33
character and personality 83-84, 164, 176
death 178
insists on negotiating with strikers 171
marriage 122-23
president of Ford Motor Company 124
relations with his father 55-56, 152, 164, 171, 176-78
Ford, Henry:
ancestors 9-14
assistants on first cars (Bishop, Huff, Julien, Wills) 34-36, 42-46, 57-62
attacks on the Jews in his newspaper 149-51
attitude toward 1929 Depression 158-59, 185
attitude toward unions 168
attitude toward his workmen 75, 185-87
birds and outdoor life 92, 122
birthplace 12-13
camera and bicycle 31-33

camping trips 142

character and personality 98-99, 176, 181-82, 185-87

controls industrial empire 131-32

creates historical museums 143-48

creates Sociological Department, Ford Motor Company 101-104, 186–87

death and funeral 182-83

driver's license from Detroit mayor 50

enters politics 125-28

forms company to make Ford cars (see Ford Motor Company) 62-65

forms company to make parts for his car 73-74

forms company to make vanadium steel 75

health 176

home life 53-56, 75-76, 84-85, 119-22

introduces eight-hour day 98

introduces five-day week 99

introduces five-dollar day 93-99

marriage 27-28

mechanical experiments, early 7-9, 29, 31, 33-37

mother's death 15

negotiates with strikers 171-72

pacifist views 108, 115-16

Peace Ship 107-14, 186, 187

publishes *Dearborn Independent* 149-51

purchases all stock in his company 124-25

purchases Lincoln Motor Company 136

rents eleven homes before building his own 49, 59-60

repairs watches 16-18, 20

requirements for his car 41, 63, 68, 78, 186

resigns as company president, in favor of Edsel 124; in favor of Henry II 180

restores Wayside Inn 141-42

school days 14-15

square dancing 148-49

sued by Dodge Brothers 123-24

sued by Sapiro for libel 150-51

sued by Selden on patent rights 69-71, 80, 82-83

sues *Chicago Tribune* for libel 133-36, 186

superintendent of Detroit Automobile Company 50

supports President Coolidge 139-40

supports President Wilson 108, 114

theater going 54

travel in Europe 84

tries to buy Independence Hall 145-46

war contracts 116-18, 173-76

Ford, Henry II, is made company president 179-81

Ford Archives 184

Ford cars:
Car Number Fifteen Million 154-55

dealers 105-106, 129

first car to run 41-45, 48, 147

first produced at factory 51-53

first sale 68-69

fourth model 53

Model A 67-68, 147

Model B 71-72

Model K 147

Model S 76

Model T 76, 77-86, 91, 147, 152-55

new Model A 147, 155-57, 159

racing cars 58-59, 60, 147

second car to run 48, 147

"Ford for President" club 139

Ford Foundation 181-82

Ford Hospital 105

Ford Motor Company
assembly line production 87-89

control by Ford family 74, 124-25
English school 103
financial success 77, 94
handicapped people hired 104-105
Highland Park plant 77-78, 85-86, 116, 187
"hunger march" at River Rouge 167-68
incorporated 65-66
labor policies 89-91, 100-101, 162
labor troubles 99-101, 166-71
Piquette Avenue plant 72
plant closed during depression 129
River Rouge plant 116
Sociological Department 101-104, 131, 186-87
strikes at River Rouge 168, 170-71
trade school 103-104
treatment of Negroes progressive 104
Willow Run plant 175
Ford Museum 145-48, 184, 187

"gas engines" (see "internal combustion engine")
gasoline car, first in U.S.A. 33
General Motors 130, 154
Greenfield Village 143-45, 187

Haynes car 33, 39
Hoover, President Herbert 145, 158

internal combustion engine patented 37-38

King, Charles Brady, tests "horseless carriage" in Detroit streets 39-42
Knudsen, William S. 72-73, 90, 130-31

Lelands of Lincoln Motor Company 136-38
Lewis, John L., organizes CIO 166-67
Lovett Hall for dancing 149

Magill's jewelry shop, watch repairing 20-22
Malcomson, Alex Y. 63-65, 74, 81
Maxim car 33, 39
Maybury, William C., Detroit mayor 50, 52
Michigan Car Company, Ford's first job in Detroit 20
Muscle Shoals 140

"New Deal" of F.D.R. 160-62

Oldfield, Barney, drives Ford's racing car 60-62
Olds car (Oldsmobile) 33, 39, 50, 52, 93
Oscar II, Peace Ship 109-14
Otto gas engine 38, 83

Philadelphia Centennial Exposition 18

Selden, George B.: patents internal combustion engine 37; "Selden buggy" 82, 147; sues Ford 69-71, 80, 82-83
Sorenson, Charles E. 72, 79-80, 87, 138, 174-75, 178-79

Tennessee Valley Authority (TVA) 141

Westinghouse steam engines 23-24
Willys-Overland Motor Company 179
Wilson, President Woodrow 108, 109, 114, 128
Winton car 33, 56-59
World wars (I) 107 ff; (II) 173 ff.

191

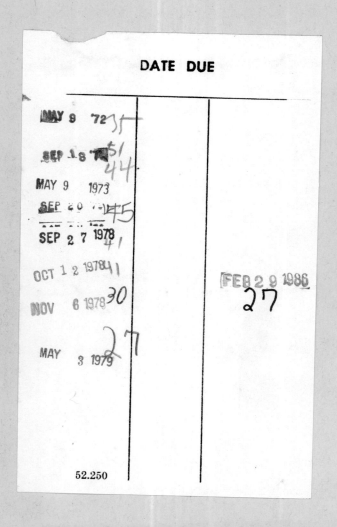